Zero to One Million

Using Real Estate to Take My Family to New Heights

By

Vendarryl Jenkins Sr

Table of Contents

Forward

In the book of Jeremiah, Chapter 29, verse 11, it says, "For I know the plans I have for you, plans to prosper you and not to harm you, plans to give you hope and a future." Yet, many men in my family have followed a different path. They adhered to a traditional narrative: securing jobs, getting married, buying homes, and raising families. However, as the years wore on, frustration and exhaustion set in, and they found themselves ensnared in the daily grind. To cope, some turned to destructive outlets—alcohol, drugs, partying, and gambling. These vices offered only fleeting relief while consuming the prime years of their lives. A few ended up behind bars, serving years they could never reclaim. These men, whom I know and love, retired broken—physically and emotionally drained.

Many of my friends have spent their entire lives within a ten-mile radius in Chicago, never truly experiencing life beyond it.

My name is Vendarryl Jenkins. I am a retired Federal Agent and spent over 20 years in real estate, buying, holding, and managing properties. Real estate wasn't just a career for me—it was my ticket to freedom. It allowed me to break the generational cycle and provide for my family in ways that improved our lifestyle. I invested in real estate to secure a future that would redefine my family's trajectory. Along the way, I traveled to over 20 countries, immersing myself in the cultures of the African diaspora. Now, at this stage in my life, I feel called to give back, mentor, and help young people grow.

I am a proud member of Alpha Phi Alpha Fraternity, Inc., the first Black Greek fraternity, which taught me the importance of servant leadership. Additionally, as a member of 100 Black Men of

America, where our motto is "They Can't Be What They Can't See," I am committed to empowering young men through mentorship. This is my message to other men: We need mentors. Young men need role models to show them what's possible and to help them dream bigger and aim higher.

I come from the Windy City of Chicago and Dixmoor (Mo-Phi). You can break free from the limitations society and circumstance impose. A single person who believes in you can change the course of your life. Be that person for someone else. Help change their future trajectory, as others have done for me.

Introduction

Preoccupied with Growing!

In this book, I'll take you on a journey of personal growth—one that has nothing to do with height. This evolution allowed me to build a fulfilling life as I'd imagined in the NBA. My confidence, my wealth, and my ability to provide for my family—all grew beyond my wildest dreams. I became the foundation that enabled my family to thrive, creating a future that went beyond the court.

As a young boy in Chicago, I was consumed by the idea of becoming tall. Every year for my birthday, I'd ask my older sister Twana to grab a ruler and mark my height on the door frame, tracking my progress year after year. By sixth grade, I hit a growth spurt, shooting up five inches to reach five foot five. That summer, I became obsessed with basketball. We had moved to a small town called Dixmoor, where most of the boys were better than me on the court. Surrounded by so many athletic kids, I knew that if I wanted to keep up, I'd have to work harder and longer.

Each morning, I'd wake up early and head to a local court for two hours, determined to improve. That's where I met Wanda—a high school player from Thornton. She was older, stronger, and far more skilled than I was, but instead of brushing me off, she took the time to teach me the game. She showed me how to refine my jump shot, transforming my clumsy push shot into a smooth, over-the-head jumper. She drilled me on the fundamentals—the essential building blocks of basketball. Under her guidance, my left-handed jump shot became a weapon, one I used as soon as I had the courage to take it.

With my growth spurt, skill development, and fundamentals in place, I made the basketball team. Not only that—I was named a starter. I could hardly believe it. "If I keep growing like this," I thought, "I'll be six-foot-five in no time."

I was blissfully unaware that genetics had already written a different script. My mom was five foot eight, and my dad was maybe a half-inch taller—they weren't exactly NBA material. Still, I clung to hope. I asked my dad if he thought I'd get tall enough to become a star. He didn't want to crush my dreams, so he encouraged me to keep practicing. To give me hope, he pointed out that my younger brother James had been shorter than me once, then shot up to six foot two practically overnight.

The following year, I entered junior high and shot up another three inches, earning a spot on the McKinley seventh-grade basketball team. I was the twelfth man off the bench on a strong team that ended up winning a state championship. Though I spent more time on the bench than on the court, it felt like the start of something big. I became a basketball fanatic, rooting for the DePaul Blue Demons when they had stars like Mark Aguirre, Terry Cummings, and Teddy Grubbs—all local Chicago players. I also followed two smooth guards from the West Side: Glenn "Doc" Rivers at Marquette and Isiah Thomas at Indiana. But as my basketball skills soared, my grades tanked—I came home with two D's and three C's.

My parents were furious.

By the middle of high school, I had only grown two more inches, and reality set in: I was going to end up only slightly taller than my father. The weight of that realization crushed me. I had been so focused on growing taller that I hadn't prepared myself for the possibility that I might never reach those extra six inches. My confidence was shattered, and with it, my dreams of basketball greatness.

But in the void left by that disappointment, something else started to grow—my grade point average. Without basketball at the center of my world, I turned my focus to academics. I read more, studied harder, and expanded my vocabulary. I became an honor roll student, and walking across the stage to receive that recognition felt better than any game-winning shot I'd ever imagined.

After high school, I joined the Air Force. One day, a friend complimented my basketball skills, and I said, "Man, I spent so many years obsessed with growing taller. When I stopped growing, I thought my dream was dead. But maybe I was just focused on the wrong kind of growth."

He looked me up and down and replied, "You've still got some growing to do. Right now, you're a skinny, frail, one-hundred-and-forty-pound kid. But you'll fill it out. You can grow in other ways—broad shoulders, a strong chest, legs to match." His words stuck with me. I started lifting weights, determined to bulk up. By the time I left the military, I'd gained twenty pounds of muscle.

It was then that I realized how narrow-minded my focus on height had been. Physical height had consumed my thoughts for so long that I hadn't stopped to consider other forms of growth. And guess what? I'm still growing.

Chapter 1
The Push and Pull

Over the years, I've met countless people curious about real estate, often asking how I got my start and what led me to become a landlord. Like many, they saw the potential but lacked the passion or courage to take that leap of faith. Interest is easy, but having the drive to act on it is a different story.

At various real estate seminars, I met people who seemed poised to dive into real estate—yet, as life happened, they pulled back, stymied by fear, low credit scores, or lack of investment income. Like most intimidating or uncomfortable ventures, getting started requires a strong push from behind and a firm pull forward. For me, that "why" became a powerful motivator, and I'll share more about that later. But, like many people, I initially looked for a sign from God to make the leap.

To take on something as daunting as real estate, you need a powerful reason—a "why" that can carry you through the challenges. It reminded me of an experience when I was fourteen, visiting family in Long Island, New York, for the summer. My two aunts lived in apartment complexes swarming with kids my age. One day, some of the neighborhood boys dared each other to jump off the 25-foot-high diving board at the public pool. While some kids refused, saying it was too dangerous, my cousin Rod and a few others took up the challenge. Rod confidently said, "My cousin and I are in for sure." As all the boys turned to look at me, I felt cornered. Wanting to fit in, I nodded and said, "Yeah, I'm in."

The day came, and as Rod and I reached the pool and saw that towering 25-foot board, I nearly passed out. All the so-called "brave" boys were hyping each other up, shouting about how they couldn't wait to make the jump. Feeling the pressure, I muttered a Chicago-style, "Shit, me too, fellas." Climbing that ladder, it felt like ten people were ahead, pulling me up, and ten more were behind, pushing me forward. There was no turning back—it felt like a death march, each step closer to something that terrified me.

When I finally got to the top, I started to panic. "I can't do this," I said, trying to find a way out. But Rod looked me in the eye and said, "There's no way down. We're here now—you have to jump." Rod was right in front of me. He grabbed my hand, looked at me with steady resolve, and said, "I know you're scared, but we've got to jump in. Let's go." And with that, he pulled me forward, and I went off that 25-foot diving board screaming.

On the way down, I felt a whirlwind of emotions—fear, regret, loss of control—mixed with a strange sense of freedom. I thought, "My mom is going to kill me for taking such a risk." My mother was conservative, always emphasizing safe, steady choices: get good grades, stay out of trouble, be respectful, and eventually, someone will want to hire you. She never once mentioned that I could build something of my own or hire others.

That leap helped me understand the value of stepping out of my comfort zone. From that moment, I became more comfortable being uncomfortable, which prepared me for the extraordinary endeavors I would later jump into.

When I finally hit the water, we plunged deep fast. My swim teacher had taught us that jumping into a pool naturally pulls you down, but if you remember the principles, stay calm, and don't panic, you can reach the surface. I kept my composure, pushing my arms down and kicking my feet, and soon, I came up, swimming away quickly as others jumped in behind us. That experience taught me an invaluable lesson: sometimes, you have to jump into the unknown, even when it terrifies you—because that's how real growth happens.

In 1997, my job as a Federal Agent transferred me and my young family from Chicago to Knoxville, Tennessee. My wife, Shafonda, our infant daughter, Arielle, and our little boy, Vendarryl Jr. (VJ), were starting a new chapter. As we settled into Knoxville, we began finding new doctors for ourselves and pediatricians for the kids. We chose Dr. Stanley Parks, a Korean pediatrician, to care for our children. After several visits with VJ, Dr. Parks requested a consultation with my wife and me. Unsure of what to expect, we arrived with a mixture of curiosity and apprehension.

To our surprise, Dr. Parks informed us that our son's cognitive development was exceptionally high. He explained that VJ would likely be a gifted learner with a need for a specialized learning environment to keep his curiosity engaged and his mind challenged. While the news was flattering, it was also daunting. As an ordinary person, I wondered, "How can I provide the right environment for such a gifted child?"

Fortunately, we discovered a Montessori school called The Giving Tree, led by a wonderful head named Maria. She fostered an environment that nurtured VJ's abilities, and he flourished there. By kindergarten, his reading and math skills were at a third-grade level. This unique school had several students working at advanced levels, some even performing at a fifth-grade level.

When a colleague invited me to a real estate seminar about buying properties and becoming a landlord, I saw an opportunity. I came home excited, sharing my new plan with my wife, Shafonda: I intended to become a real estate investor to afford VJ the best schooling possible. I began devouring every resource I could find—books like Rich Dad Poor Dad, Who Moved My Cheese, and autobiographies of people who took bold leaps of faith to achieve extraordinary success. Yet, despite my enthusiasm, fear lingered. As a young man with a wife, two children, two cars, and a newly constructed home, our finances were stretched thin.

In 1999, during a Jenkins family reunion in Mobile, Alabama, I was introduced to my father's first cousin, Spencer Jenkins. Though Spencer was technically my cousin, I knew him more through family whispers about his substantial real estate wealth in Washington, D.C. Intrigued, I shared my aspirations of becoming a real estate investor. Spencer encouraged me to visit him in Washington, where he believed he could help with my plans. We exchanged contact information, and I left the reunion feeling optimistic about having found a valuable ally.

One year later, my job notified me that my family and I would be relocating to Washington, D.C., known affectionately as Chocolate City. Overjoyed, I called Spencer to let him know I was on my way and eager to start my real estate investment journey.

Once we arrived, we settled in the scenic town of Bristow, Virginia, just outside of D.C. Known for its top-tier public schools, Virginia seemed ideal for VJ's education. We enrolled him in Bristow Run Elementary and decided to wait until the parent-teacher conference to discuss his academic needs. We hoped the teacher would recognize his talents and recommend him for the gifted program.

However, during the conference, we were met with an unexpected response. VJ's first-grade teacher didn't believe he needed to be in the gifted program. She remarked, "Mr. Jenkins, every parent believes their child is gifted—until reality shows them otherwise." Her words stung but also fueled my determination. I knew then that I would do whatever it took to get my son into a private school that could nurture his potential.

We began working with VJ at home, buying books and consulting with his former Montessori school for resources. Yet, during the next year's conference, while the new teacher acknowledged that VJ was ahead of his peers, she assigned him the role of "teacher's helper," assisting other students to catch up rather than challenging him. Frustrated, I felt a growing urgency to find the specialized education he needed.

Around this time, Spencer reached out with a proposal to help kickstart my real estate journey. He explained that many new landlords struggle with the maintenance costs that eat into rental income. Spencer suggested a unique solution: he had arranged for me to work weekends as a maintenance worker at a high-rise apartment complex in Maryland. When I voiced my concern, saying, "I don't know anything about apartment maintenance," Spencer replied, "That's why I told them you'd work for free for a couple of months." He explained that this hands-on experience would teach me how to handle common maintenance issues—knowledge that would be invaluable once I owned my own properties.

Spencer emphasized that working in maintenance would allow me to learn how to handle common issues in rental units, easing some of my fears about becoming a landlord. I promptly bought coveralls and boots and started my new role. As a Federal Agent, I had done my share of undercover work, but this was a different kind of immersion—posing as a maintenance man in a 100-unit apartment building. Monday through Friday, I was in a suit and tie at headquarters; on weekends, I became part of the maintenance team.

The guys I worked with were great, especially the man training me. Every Saturday morning, we'd grab a stack of maintenance tickets and a grocery cart filled with tools and replacement parts. My trainer explained that each unit had the same brand of fixtures, the same paint colors, and the same flooring, making repairs relatively straightforward. He taught me quick fixes for clogged sinks and tubs (often due to hair), as well as simple repairs for stoves and refrigerators. Occasionally, we'd need to order parts and return later, but I was surprised by how much we could diagnose and fix with experience alone.

After three months, I was offered a paid position on the maintenance team. I appreciated the gesture, but I knew I was ready to take the next step and buy my first property. Through Spencer, I met several real estate agents who began showing me potential properties. I eventually made a deal on a four-unit building at 3301 D Street SE in Washington, D.C. During my due diligence, I had an inspection done on all units and felt confident discussing the findings with the inspector. The foundation was solid, the electrical systems were separately metered, and the plumbing was in excellent shape. Since four-plex and duplex buildings are classified as residential, financing was easier, allowing me to purchase the property with a small down payment. I planned to use the rent from two units to cover expenses, while the income from the other two would go toward my family's goals.

Before closing, Shafonda and I drove by the property. Smiling, she said, "Vendarryl, you did it." I replied, "This is just the beginning—we're going to get VJ out of public school." At that point, VJ was in third grade and had finally been assigned a teacher who recognized his abilities. She questioned why he hadn't been placed in the gifted program earlier and promised to help him access advanced work. We appreciated her support but remained focused on moving VJ to the best school we could afford.

One Saturday, while at a youth sports event, another parent approached me. He mentioned he was on the board of The Wakefield School in Plains, Virginia, a private institution known for academic excellence. The parent explained that the school was looking for talented students who could bring diversity. After researching, I discovered that the tuition was steep.

To add to the challenge, our daughter Airielle, who had been just a toddler during Dr. Stanley Parks' consultation, was now five. The Wakefield School had a combined elementary, middle, and high school, so I arranged for both children to be tested for admission. I also met with Headmaster Peter Quinn, explaining, "Sir, I was told my son has the potential to attend an Ivy League school. If his test scores indicate that promise to you, I'd like your help in getting him there. I don't know all the classes or books he'll need, but I believe your team does." I added, "My daughter Airielle also tested today. While no one has indicated she should be in a gifted program, she's a hardworking girl with her own unique strengths."

When the results came back, VJ scored in the high 90th percentile, and Airielle placed in the 70th percentile. The school offered VJ an almost full scholarship, while I would pay full tuition for Airielle. I was thrilled because, while my plan had always been to secure VJ a quality education, I couldn't imagine one child having more opportunities than the other. It was settled—VJ would start fourth grade, and Airielle would start first grade at Wakefield.

On their first day, as I watched them in their navy-blue blazers adorned with the Wakefield Owl crest, I felt an overwhelming sense of pride. I had made a long-term plan and, against all odds, stuck to it. With the rental income from my properties, I was able to cover their tuition. Around this time, my wife, Shafonda, and I celebrated our ten-year anniversary, smiling at how everything was falling into place for our young family.

The school had just begun at The Wakefield School when we received a call from the high school basketball coach. He told us about a young man from the Virgin Islands who had come to play basketball and pursue a good education. The young man needed a family to take him in.

Initially, we were hesitant. We had a young daughter, and our son, VJ, was still very young. Bringing a high school-aged boy into our home felt like a big step. However, after some deliberation, we decided to meet with him. We were immediately impressed; he was well-mannered, mature, and carried himself with a calm confidence. We thought he could be a positive influence and a good big brother to VJ, who was known for his mischievous streak.

We decided to welcome Eric Wilson into our home, becoming his guardians so he could benefit from the same opportunities our kids were receiving. With three children now enrolled in this prestigious academic school, I knew I had to make my real estate investment work. Success wasn't just a goal—it was essential.

Our beautiful home in Virginia, where Shafonda and I raised our kids

Chapter 2
That Chicago Shit

At the real estate closing table, I reflected on how grateful I was for the books I'd read and the seminars I'd attended on buying investment properties. But as I sat there, I realized that none of those resources had truly prepared me for the challenges I was about to face as a novice landlord. With so many people counting on my success, I was determined to win—at any cost. Little did I know just how much danger, financial strain, and sacrifice this education would demand.

Before diving into the journey of becoming a competent landlord in Southeast D.C., let me share some background. I offer this not because you need the same experiences to succeed, but to provide insight into the influences that shaped my decisions—the successes and costly mistakes. Our perspectives on life are often molded by the environments in which we're raised.

I grew up in Chicago, raised by my mother, Annetter, and my father, Bobby, in the same home—a rarity at that time. My parents had moved from rural Alabama to escape the hardships there, where most people worked in cotton fields, ran moonshine, or lived as sharecroppers. I was the only boy, sandwiched between my older sister, Twana, and my younger sister, Lashawn.

When we moved to a small house in the south suburbs, I attended high school in a rough area just outside Chicago called Harvey. Growing up in an urban environment gave me valuable insight into the types of people I would later encounter as tenants.

You never know the struggles people are carrying in those communities until you meet them. Alongside these lessons, I learned the unwritten rules and behaviors that come with surviving in Chicago. Tempers flared easily, and violence often erupted without much warning.

In Chicago's schools, dismissal was always at 3:15 p.m., and when a conflict brewed, you'd often hear someone declare, "3:15, motherfucker!" That phrase, "motherfucker," was the most potent expletive we learned outside the classroom, and a "3:15" meant you were being challenged to a fight after school.

As a slightly built kid, I wasn't usually the challenger, and I tried to avoid fights whenever I could. But a few times, I had no choice but to defend myself. One unforgettable experience happened when I was twelve; I couldn't escape a confrontation and ended up being knocked out cold in the street by a sixteen-year-old.

The turning point that triggered my "aggressive switch" and taught me to stand up for myself happened in high school. Early in my freshman year, an upperclassman started bullying me. I tried to stand my ground, asking him to leave me alone, but he responded by punching me in the chest and arms, and I backed down. This went on for several days until my friend EC, whom I'd known since grade school, said, "V, man, you've got to fight this guy back."

Another older boy from my neighborhood put it even more bluntly: "Vendarryl, if you don't fight back, you'll be like a young 'vagina' for these bullies to pass around. Once he's bored, he'll just hand you off to the next guy." His words stung deeply and lit a fire within me. I decided I was never going to be bullied like that again.

I went home that night, stood in front of my bedroom mirror, and practiced punching combinations, resolved that I would land at least two solid hits, no matter the consequences. The next day, I walked into school with my mind made up. In the boy's locker room, the bully came up behind me and sneered, "Move out of the way, pussy." I spun around and hit him with a right hook, then my hardest left punch.

It knocked him back, but it didn't knock him out. Furious, he shouted, "I'm going to kill you, motherfucker!" and unleashed a barrage of punches, knocking me into the lockers. When I fell, he tried to stomp me, but a few older boys stepped in, pulling him off. I heard them saying, "Enough is enough—he doesn't weigh but 130 pounds."

I got up, blood dripping from my mouth, where my lip had embedded into my braces. An older guy patted me on the back and said, "That's the way to stand up for yourself, shorty." The same older boys who had previously watched me get bullied now gave me approving nods. EC walked with me to the nurse's office and said, "See, I told you—stand up to a bully, and they'll stop."

From then on, anytime I faced bullying, something snapped within me, bringing me back to that moment. It was a switch that could take me from 0 to 100 in an instant.

Growing up in an urban environment like mine meant being exposed to more violence than any child should have to face—rapes, homicides, robberies, and other brutalities. It forces you to mature too quickly. For us in Chicago, life lessons came from watching the 10:00 p.m. news with our parents. Every night, there was another tragedy, and you couldn't help but mentally prepare for the worst.

My parents would turn those violent headlines into teachable moments. "You don't always get a second chance to be young and dumb, so learn from this," they'd warn, emphasizing that life didn't often grant do-overs.

After a stint in the United States Air Force, I attended Chicago State University, right in the heart of the South Side. Commuting to and from school exposed me to all kinds of risks—getting robbed and having guns and knives pulled on me. Sometimes, it felt like I wouldn't survive the journey. During this time, I also worked at my dad's tire store on 47th and State, next to the Robert Taylor housing projects. My dad believed that if I worked hard doing a gritty, hands-on job like changing tires, I'd push myself harder in school to build a different future. That period in my life taught me a lot about people, resilience, and survival in tough circumstances.

Once, I wrote an essay about the people I'd come to know around 47th Street. My professor gave me an A and commented, "Your imaginary characters feel so real." I replied, "They're real. They're people society has forgotten." I eventually went on to earn a Master's in Criminal Justice from the University of Wisconsin-Platteville.

When I graduated, my mother's dream came true: I had done well in school, avoided drugs and crime, and finally, someone wanted to hire me. And it wasn't just any job—it was a position most people only dream about. I became a Federal Agent. My first assignment was in Northwest Indiana, where we worked heavily in areas like Gary, Hammond, and East Chicago. Gary, though smaller, had many of the same challenges as Chicago but with even fewer opportunities for young men.

When I started my career in federal law enforcement, I weighed just 160 pounds and barely passed my firearm qualification. Trying to gain the trust of my mostly White, aggressive, Type-A colleagues forced me to push myself and become more assertive. Twice a year, we hit the mats for wrestling and combat training. That pressure not only toughened me up physically but also sharpened my ability to adapt and survive in any environment.

I hit the shooting range twice a week and the gym five days a week, relentlessly pushing weights. Over three years, I transformed into a near-perfect marksman and packed on 25 pounds of muscle. Bench pressing 295 pounds and squatting 350 pounds unleashed a certain aggression—a drive to show people just how strong I had become. Working in law enforcement in places like Gary, Indiana, and Chicago, where gang members and criminals were abundant, provided ample opportunities to put those skills to real-life use.

One Friday, my wife, Shafonda, and I had just left the closing for our first real estate property, located at 3301 D Street in Washington, D.C. We decided to celebrate with dinner at one of our favorite spots. The next morning, we gathered the kids, drove to the building, and let them walk around in the vacant unit. In hindsight, this was the calm before the storm—a moment of peace before a series of trials that would test me on every level.

Wasting no time, Shafonda and I put our business degrees to work, drafting new rental agreements and outlining payment procedures. Four days after closing, I went to the property after work to introduce myself to the tenants and explain some of the changes we'd be implementing. Everything was going smoothly as I tried to build rapport and meet the families in the building. Then, around 6:30 p.m., one of the tenants came upstairs and said, "Mr. Jenkins, you'd better leave quickly before the real landlords show up."

Confused, I asked, "What do you mean?"

She replied, "Around 7:00, drug dealers come here, and they sell drugs in the building. They don't let us come out of our apartments."

I felt a sinking feeling in my gut. During my due diligence, I'd never thought to check on the property at night. Dressed in a suit and trench coat from my workday, I realized I had a choice: I could leave as advised, call the police, or stand my ground, Chicago style.

I sat by a window, watching and gathering my thoughts. Sure enough, around 7:15, four young men strolled up to the property, laughing and talking with an air of confidence. For thirty more minutes, I debated calling the police, but ultimately, I decided to confront them myself.

I walked downstairs, and as I approached, one of them shouted, "Get your ass back in your unit before you get dealt with."

I opened my trench coat to reveal my badge on one side and my gun on the other. I said, "Gentlemen, we have a problem we need to solve tonight. We're all entrepreneurs here, but only one of us is paying utilities, taxes, and a mortgage to make money here. My name is Mr. Jenkins. I just closed on this building last week, and I plan to be here for a long time."

The young men squared up, taking aggressive stances. One of them sneered, "You must be crazy if you think you're going to run us off by yourself. We're going to kill you tonight."

I replied, "That may be true, but I promise you, I'm not alone. I've got thirteen friends in my clip and one in the chamber, and I'll start with the one in your head. I'm a federal agent, and I can guarantee I'll take down at least two of you. The other two? Even if I don't get you tonight, tomorrow, everyone's going to know who you are, where you live, and what went down here."

I continued, "All I'm asking is that you move your operation from my building. A Federal Agent and drug dealers can't co-exist here. It's insane to think we can."

The youngest one tensed up, breathing fast. "Let's kill him," he muttered.

I placed my hand on my gun. "You'd better get this young motherfucker in line," I warned. "I'm from Chicago, and I don't do a lot of back and forth."

One of the older men gave me a long look, then said, "Let's go. You got it, Po Po."

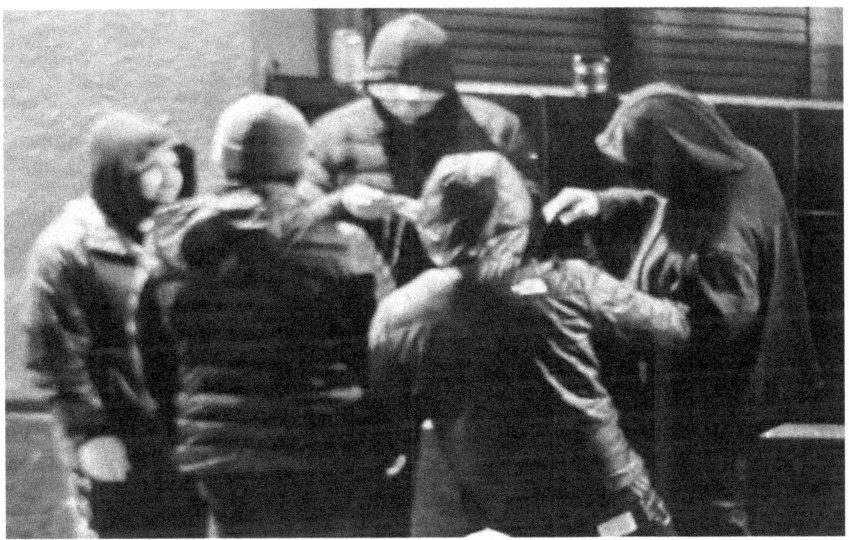

I went back upstairs, trembling as I tried to gather myself. I muttered under my breath, "That was the dumbest thing you've ever done." Here I was, a husband and father, acting like some street thug from Chicago. I sat there for hours, berating myself until it dawned on me: without proper training, you always fall back on what's familiar. That kid who mouthed off to me had become the high school bully I'd faced down in the locker room. And at that moment, I was ready to shoot him in the head.

When I got home and told my South Side of Chicago wife what happened, she sighed and said, "You should have called the police, baby." Then, with a forgiving smile, she held out her hand and said, "But what did you tell them, baby? We don't do a whole lot of talking back and forth in Chicago." I gave her a high five, and we hugged. But I knew deep down that I'd let her down with those street antics, and I needed to stay out of those situations going forward. If I wasn't careful, I could lose everything.

Soon, the seventh of the month rolled around, and I went to check the rented mailbox at the post office. Not a single rent check. The only payment I'd received was from the Section 8 tenant, whose rent was deposited directly into my account. I had one vacant unit and two tenants who hadn't paid. After work, I went to the building, knocked on their doors, and met with blunt refusals to pay. One tenant even told me they'd had a meeting and decided they didn't like me. They figured that if they withheld rent, I'd run out of money and be forced to sell the building.

I called the previous owner and asked him about the rent history, and he admitted that those two tenants hadn't paid rent in four months. Furious, I returned to the building, knocked on their doors, and told them I wanted to look them in the eyes as I promised to go to court the next day and start the process of kicking their no-good asses to the street.

Having good credit is crucial when starting any business, especially real estate. I went to my bank and secured a $5,000 personal bridge loan—essentially, temporary funds to get through a tough spot. I had my first experience with the landlord-tenant court system, which, in Washington, D.C., was heavily pro-tenant. I would strongly suggest that anyone investing in real estate spend time understanding the local court system as part of their due diligence.

My cousin Spencer shared a well-known method for getting tenants out in the D.C. area. He explained that in D.C., evictions typically aren't carried out in winter or early spring, when temperatures are below 60 degrees. That means tenants can live rent-free for four to six months. He said, "Do the math, college boy. Offer them a thousand dollars and moving expenses, and they might leave in 30 days. That's cheaper than losing thousands in rent and legal fees."

I replied, "Sounds good, but I just told them I was putting them out, and we exchanged some heated words." He shook his head and said, "Go back and smooth things over. That was dumb."

Taking his advice, I returned to the building and sat down with the two tenants to make my pitch. I had mixed success—one tenant accepted the offer, but the other one refused, which meant I had to go through court and wait four months to evict her.

That was my first costly lesson as a property manager.

Things didn't go quite as planned with the tenant, who had agreed to leave. She called me and said, "Mr. Jenkins, I was planning to move out, but I'm having a problem with my boyfriend." Surprised, I replied, "What boyfriend? You're the only one on the lease." She explained, "I just started seeing this guy, and he moved in. Now he doesn't want to leave."

I now had what was essentially a squatter in my apartment—someone illegally staying there without my permission. After consulting an attorney, I learned I'd have to go to tenant court to have him evicted. Facing the possibility that he could stay for six or seven months, I decided to try talking to him directly, hoping I could negotiate his departure with a bit of cash.

I went to the apartment, used my key to enter, and pretended to be shocked to see him there. "Jennifer is gone," I said, "so why are you still here?"

He leaned back, cool as ice, and said, "I've decided I'm going to live here as long as I want, Mr. Jenkins. Now, if you don't mind, I'd like to watch my TV."

I left, seething. As I drove around D.C., trying to cool off, I called a buddy from Chicago, another agent who worked at headquarters with me. I told him what had happened, and he immediately offered to help. "Come get me, and we'll take care of this," he said. It sounded tempting at first, but two Chicago guys handling this? Probably not the wisest move.

When I picked him up, he came out of his house with a short-barrel shotgun, a black leather jacket, and a ski mask. I shook my head, "What are you doing, robbing a liquor store? Leave that shotgun in the car, man."

He reluctantly agreed, and we headed to the building. I used my key to get inside. The squatter saw us and smirked. "Mr. Jenkins, if you don't get out of my apartment, I'm gonna get my thing from under the bed and hurt you and your boy."

I grabbed my friend's arm. Craig was 6'3" and 220 pounds, and, like me, he wasn't big on words. "We're not scared," I told him, "but I brought him to make sure nothing goes wrong."

The guy started counting down, "Five…four…three…" But before he reached "two," I rushed him. He spun around, reaching for something under the bed. I tackled him, lifted him, and slammed him to the ground. Straddling him, I punched him until I felt Craig pulling me off. The squatter scrambled for his phone, yelling, "I'm calling the police!"

I laughed. "This is my building, and I am the police. I'm not going anywhere."

We sat in the living room, having found a stash of guns under the mattress. When the D.C. police arrived, we identified ourselves as federal agents and explained the situation. One of the officers, clearly unimpressed, asked, "Where are you brothers from? This doesn't look like official police business."

I smirked and replied, "Chicago. This guy's a squatter, and he tried to pull weapons on us."

The D.C. officer pulled me aside. "Look, man, I'm from Cleveland, and my partner's from D.C. We know the game. We're doing you a solid this time, but you'd better change your management style before you get yourself in trouble." Then he turned to the squatter and said, "You've got guns and ammo in D.C., so we have to take you in."

The squatter protested, "But I called the police on them!"

The officers cuffed him, took him to their squad car, and returned to us. "Hurry up and change those locks," they said, giving us a nod. "We've extended all the professional courtesy we can, fellas."

Craig and I went to Home Depot, bought some locks, and changed them that night. As I drove Craig home, we couldn't help but laugh. "This is some crazy Chicago shit," we said, knowing it was far from professional. After I dropped him off, I knew the D.C. police were right: I needed to change my approach to property management.

I talked to my cousin Spencer, and he introduced me to a landlord mentor who owned buildings near mine in Southeast D.C. I also signed up for a two-day property management seminar in North Carolina. If I wanted to expand and buy more properties, I had to improve my tenant management skills or hire a professional management company. For a while, I tried outsourcing to a property management company, but I wasn't making enough to cover their fees. Plus, my wife, Shafonda, a control-freak accountant, didn't trust anyone else handling our money. And to be honest, you have to manage the management companies, or they'll take advantage of you if you don't provide oversight.

When Christmas came, we went back to Chicago to spend time with family and friends. At our family's Christmas Eve party, I was surprised to see my cousin Derrick, recently out of jail, laughing and talking with everyone. Sometimes, he kept his distance because of my law enforcement career, but that night, he came over and shared some wisdom. "Cuz," he said, "I've learned something inside. You can't control the thoughts and impulses that come into your head, but with education and counseling, you can control which ones you act on."

His words hit me hard, given everything I'd been dealing with. I laughed, hugged him, and said, "I'm glad to see you out. Now stay out this time, alright?"

On my way to my in-laws' house that night, I thought to myself, I'm more educated than most, yet I'm still struggling to control these impulses. Right then, I decided it was time to drop all that Chicago street mentality and use my mind to outmaneuver my tenants.

Chapter 3
Loosing Spencer

After the first six months, things started to smooth out at my first investment property on D Street. We were loving everything about living in Northern Virginia, just outside of D.C. There are advantages and disadvantages to living close to your investment properties. I lived about 45 minutes away from mine, which gave me time to mellow out before getting home to my family. I knew in the back of my mind that, for me to execute my long-term goal of giving my kids the best education, I would need to stay in Virginia for a while.

I often marveled at how blessed I was to have lived out so many of my childhood dreams, including my real estate investments. Surprisingly, living in Virginia had been one of those dreams. My first friend in Chicago, JG, had a mother who was from Richmond, Virginia. Back in elementary school, he used to show me pictures of his summer vacations spent visiting his family in Virginia. He had snapshots from Colonial Williamsburg, Historic Jamestowne, Yorktown Settlement, and Monticello. To a city boy like me, those places looked like a whole different world.

JG used to tell me how much he loved Virginia, saying, "Virginia's got so many different identities. From Richmond, you can drive two hours east and hit the beach, two hours west and reach the mountains, two hours south and be deep in the countryside, or head two hours north and find yourself in Chocolate City—Washington, D.C." He always said that when he finished school, he was going to move to Virginia. I remember thinking, *If it's the last*

I tracked down JG's old phone number, and to my surprise, he was still living in Chicago. I told him that I had made it to Northern Virginia. He was happy to hear from me, though saddened that life hadn't led him to Virginia as he had once hoped. JG said, "Man, Vendarryl, life happened, and I kind of lost my way." I told him, "It's not over yet. You've just hit a delay, JG."

Since things were running smoothly with the building, I started spending more time with my cousin Spencer during my downtime. He was quite the character, full of knowledge, and I soaked it up like a sponge. Most of the family didn't know the deeper details of his life that he was now sharing with me. Despite being somewhat of a family superhero, I quickly realized he was a flawed human being, just like me—a man God had shown favor to.

Spencer was a mechanical genius. He could dismantle a huge boiler system into its smallest parts, figure out the problem, and then put it all back together perfectly. He had grown up as a poor sharecropper in lower Alabama, with only a sixth-grade education. He spoke about his family's hardships—how often they went to bed hungry, only to wake up the next day and work from sunup to sundown. Every Thanksgiving, he catered a huge feast for his siblings, allowing them to enjoy the abundance they never had as kids. "It brings me joy," he said, "to know that, at least for that one day, nobody's hungry and everybody can eat until they're full."

I asked Spencer, "What made you choose the D.C. area to settle down in?"

Spencer said that when he was young and reckless, he was jealous and abusive toward a woman he had two kids with. He told me that the woman left him with the kids in Alabama and moved to New York City. After some time, he decided to head to New York to reconnect with them, but his car broke down in D.C. With little money, he decided to get a job to fix his car before continuing his journey.

I called him out on that part of the story, teasing, "Something must have caught your eye and made you stay in Chocolate City for a while." We both laughed. He admitted that a woman had taken him to the building where she worked and helped him get a maintenance job there.

The building was owned by a white Jewish man and featured those enormous boiler systems you could walk inside. Spencer started working under the engineering supervisor responsible for maintaining the boilers. Back then, you had to be a licensed engineer to work on those massive systems, which required passing a test. Spencer quickly became an expert on the boilers.

"I got so good," he said, "that the building owner paid my supervisor to take the test for me." And just like that, Spencer became a licensed engineer, despite having only a sixth-grade education. That certification opened doors for him, and people began paying him well to work on their boilers. Over time, Spencer got to know several wealthy real estate investors. As they grew older and no longer wanted certain properties, they'd sell him small buildings at a discount.

Spencer met his wife, Veronica, just as she was about to start medical school. Her sister worked as a cleaner in the apartment building where Spencer was employed. One day, the sister told him, "My sister Veronica just graduated from Howard University, and she's looking for a part-time job cleaning apartments to help pay for medical school."

Shortly after, Spencer and Veronica began dating, and before long, he was helping her with her medical school expenses. They eventually got married, and Spencer fully supported her through medical school. They were quite the odd couple, but always a joy to be around. Spencer used to joke when they argued, calling her "stupid," and Veronica would fire back, "I went to medical school, and I'm stupid, huh?" He'd laugh and reply, "Well, I paid for your medical school, so clearly, I'm smarter than you, my dear."

They'd share a laugh over it—the idea of a poor sharecropper from Alabama being sent by God to Washington, D.C., to fund her medical education was always a source of amusement. I couldn't help but think this was a perfect example of how God can send anyone, from any walk of life, to be a blessing.

Over the next six months, Spencer started to become sick more often, and we weren't able to hang out as much. One day, he called me and said, "Cuz, come pick me up from my house." I went over to Maryland where he lived and found him in bed, struggling to get up.

I asked, "Spencer, are you okay?"

He said, "I'll be fine, Cuz. Give me a few more minutes."

After he got ready, we started driving and ended up at an apartment building located at 2501 Naylor Road Southeast, D.C.

He said, "This man I did some work for just passed away, and his family wants to sell some of his buildings. They're willing to hold a note on a nine-unit building."

Up to that point, I thought all mortgages were handled through banks or financial institutions. I wasn't familiar with the idea of someone personally holding a promissory note and the buyer making payments directly to them. Spencer explained, "The family owns the property free and clear, and they're looking to sell it for $225,000. They want $25,000 as a down payment and will finance the remaining $200,000 at 7% interest." He continued, "The loan is for 30 years, but it can be paid off or refinanced after five years. So, while the payments are spread over 30 years, I can pay it off early if I choose."

He said, "Go in and look over the building for me with this guy I'm supposed to meet." At first, I thought the building was for him, but then I realized he was trusting me to evaluate the nine-unit property on his behalf because he wasn't feeling well.

I went in, and the guy showed me around. I inspected the electrical systems, heating, apartment layouts, and even went up on the roof.

About an hour later, I came back to the car. Spencer was asleep, but when he woke up, he asked, "What do you think about the building?"

I replied, "Man, you'll have a nice building."

Then Spencer asked, "How much of the $25,000 can you come up with right now?"

I responded, "Cuz, the most I can manage is around $5,000, and I'd need to talk to my wife about moving money around. I'm only twelve months into this game—I'm not ready for a nine-unit building."

Spencer chuckled and said, "I believe in you. I'm only upset you didn't get to D.C. sooner." He paused, then added, "Think about it. But before you take me home, I need to stop by the bank."

"Sure thing, no problem, Spencer," I said.

About twenty minutes later, he came out of the bank holding a cashier's check made out to me. Handing it to me, he said, "Here's the lawyer's number. If you can come up with the $5,000, you've got yourself a building."

I protested, "I can't accept this much money from you, Spencer."

But he responded, "I didn't say it was a gift—it's a loan. Veronica will draw up a promissory note for $20,000 at zero percent interest."

Spencer's move got me thinking more about seller financing. Sometimes sellers will offer owner financing because they want to sell the property at a higher price than its appraisal value, and buyers agree to soft terms on the loan. It can also provide a huge tax-saving benefit because the seller only pays taxes on the amount received from monthly payments. Others use it as a way to keep cash flow coming in monthly, just as they had when they owned the property. In some cases, owner financing is used to incentivize the sale of a hard-to-sell property by making it easy to obtain.

I went home, excited to share the news with my wife, Shafonda. However, she wasn't as thrilled about the idea of taking on a nine-unit building.

"Vendarryl," she said, "you're just getting comfortable managing a four-unit property, and now you're jumping into something much bigger. A nine-unit building?"

Shafonda and I had been together for a long time, so I understood her thought process well. She's naturally cautious, and I knew better than to push her. Instead, I let her process the information on her own. She always starts by thinking of every possible worst-case scenario, consults her father and uncle, and ultimately comes back with a list of questions and demands.

Three days later, she approached me and said, "I'm still uncertain, but take me to see the building."

I called the realtor to arrange another showing and told him to get a contract ready. The realtor emphasized that we needed to move quickly because other investors were showing interest. I explained to Shafonda that we would sign the contract with a 45-day due diligence clause. I reassured her, "This clause allows us to professionally inspect the property, review rent rolls, leases, or anything else. If it doesn't meet our standards, we can walk away from the deal without losing a penny."

She moaned and groaned about marrying a man who always wanted to take risks and put the family at risk. I laughed and said, "That's why I call you 'Doubting Debbie.' You always see the worst-case scenario in every situation."

In truth, we balanced each other out. I was always optimistic, envisioning the best-case scenario, while she brought potential risks to my attention. One of her demands was for me to put together a business plan detailing how I would manage the additional nine units, keep my job, and still spend time with the family.

To address her concerns, I began formulating a team to help with the building and tenants. That's when I met Mr. B. He had been cutting the grass for the previous property owner on D Street, and I hired him to stay on. Mr. B introduced me to a few more handymen in the area, and I added a couple of guys I already knew.

Then I connected with a sharp, young Black entrepreneur who owned a property management company. He was a Howard University graduate hustling in Southeast D.C., just like me. Having grown up in D.C., living in apartments himself, he had an innate understanding of how tenants wanted to live. We clicked instantly.

"If there's one thing I know," he said, "it's how to keep tenants happy."

His life experiences gave him a unique empathy for his tenants, and he introduced me to several social organizations that needed housing for their clients. These organizations provided housing for battered women, individuals recovering from substance abuse, veterans, and HIV patients. Establishing relationships with these organizations was a game changer because they guaranteed rent payments for their clients.

The property manager also provided me with essential forms, documents, updates on D.C. housing laws, and other tricks of the trade.

Through my mentor, I met an electrician, a painter, an exterminator, and a plumber. I outlined my plans to purchase more units and proposed working agreements with them. I explained that I wanted to trust them to handle issues beyond my expertise. My plan was simple: if a tenant called with a problem, Mr. B would assess the situation and inform me of the issue. If a tradesman was needed, I'd call one of them to handle it. Once the work was completed, they'd send me a picture of the repair, and the tenant would sign off that it was done. I would meet the tradesmen every Saturday to settle payments.

After addressing all of Shafonda's questions and meeting her demands, she finally agreed to move forward with the nine-unit building.

The closing for 2501 Naylor Road was straightforward. Everything was handled by the seller's attorney, so I never even met the five siblings I was paying the mortgage to. I was given a name for the checks and an address to mail them to. Veronica provided the promissory note for the loan from Spencer, so I was all set to close on my second property in less than two years.

Owner financing is quite common with commercial buildings for several reasons. Sellers often prefer it to secure a higher price than the property's appraised value. It can also provide significant tax benefits, as sellers only pay taxes on the amount they receive through monthly payments. Additionally, some sellers use owner financing to keep a steady cash flow or to make a hard-to-sell property more appealing.

Meanwhile, I busied myself putting my management plan in place at my new building. The property was 90% occupied, which meant I was immediately generating a $2,000 monthly profit. The one vacant unit was assigned to Mr. B as compensation for his work, which included mopping hallways, cutting the grass at my properties, and addressing tenant issues. I felt a deep sense of accomplishment, having managed to accumulate 13 units in just two years in the real estate investment game.

One day, while performing maintenance in one of the top units, I had a stunning view straight down Pennsylvania Avenue, showcasing the monuments. It was a remarkable experience to own a property with such a historic view.

Everything was starting to fall into place, and my property management program was working very well. One evening, my phone rang, and I recognized Spencer's number. I answered, "Hey Cuz, what's up?"

Instead of Spencer's voice, I heard his wife, Veronica. She said, "Vennie, Spencer is gone. He has died."

I was stunned. "Oh no," I said, shocked. I knew he had been sick recently, but he never told me he was that ill.

Veronica continued, "He wanted you to get another building because he felt like you might turn back without him around."

I had never experienced the death of someone so close to me before, and it was a new and difficult adjustment. I felt scared and abandoned. Spencer was the one person in this business I looked up to and knew I could count on to come to my rescue.

The aftermath of his funeral was an eye-opener for me. People came out of the woodwork, approaching Veronica, claiming Spencer wanted them to have this or that. Thankfully, Spencer had put all his properties in a trust, so Veronica didn't have to deal with the headaches of probate.

Probate is the general administration of a deceased person's assets to ensure they are distributed according to the will or estate plan. In contrast, a **trust** is a legal arrangement in which the owner of assets, including cash, securities, and real estate, transfers ownership to other entities or beneficiaries.

It took me a few months to regain my footing. Determined to make Spencer proud, I continued my journey toward reaching my potential. I established my own property management company, with my wife handling the accounting. Mr. B and several other trusted individuals managed maintenance and tenant relations. They became instrumental in helping me move forward after Spencer's death.

During challenging times, you discover who is truly willing to support you, and my team stepped up admirably.

In my experience, even the best landlords will encounter issues with about 20% of their tenants. During my initial visits to meet my tenants on Naylor Road, I immediately identified two potential problems.

One tenant knew I was coming and invited me into his unit. To my surprise, he had turned his living room into a two-seat barbershop. He and his partner had two clients in barber chairs, while four more people sat waiting for their turn.

I was so taken aback that it took me a moment to process what I was seeing. Finally, I asked if I could speak to him in the hallway.

"Sir," I said, "you cannot run a full-fledged barbershop business in your apartment. It looks like you're even collecting booth rent from another barber who's not on the lease."

He replied, "Look, Mr. Jenkins, I only cut on the weekends when I'm off work. Everything is negotiable. I didn't want to hide it from you, so what's the cut you need to turn your head?"

I told him firmly, "This isn't allowed under your lease, and I won't turn my head. However, I will make a compromise. You alone can cut your friends' hair on Saturdays—just one day a week—but your other barber has to go."

Sometimes, I feel that if you're totally inflexible, tenants will find a way to do the wrong thing anyway. By compromising, I was able to minimize the issue.

On the same day, I visited a second-floor unit and met a well-dressed, light-skinned woman who was very flirtatious and complimentary about my achievement of owning buildings. As we talked, I pointed out that, according to the rent roll I received before purchasing the property, she was a month behind on her rent. She admitted she was waiting for money from her father and promised to pay soon. I told her to contact me as soon as the money arrived because she was close to being two months behind.

A week later, she called me on a Saturday afternoon and asked if I could come by at 7:00 p.m. to pick up her rent money when she got off work. I had a feeling something wasn't quite right, so I asked my wife to ride with me. When we arrived, my wife stayed downstairs on the first floor while I went upstairs to the second floor and knocked on the tenant's door.

After a few knocks, she came to the door, stuck her head out, and said, "I just got out of the shower—hold on."

She left the door cracked and called out, "Just come on in and let me get the money."

When I pushed the door open, all I saw were her yellow cheeks bouncing as she ran back to her room. I stayed by the door, shaking my head, when she shouted from her room, "Mr. Jenkins, come back here and get your money!"

I responded, "Sweetheart, my wife is waiting for me downstairs to take this money to the bank. The currency you're offering isn't negotiable at the bank."

A few moments later, she came out in a robe and said, "Can you come back tomorrow without her? This is the way I think we can come to an agreement."

I looked at her firmly and said, "No, ma'am. I don't play with my money. This is how I pay for my kids' school. If you can't pay your rent, it would be best for you to move out."

Realizing I wouldn't succumb to her advances, she eventually moved out.

That experience taught me a valuable lesson and gave me a new mantra: **"When tenants fail to pay their rent, they're effectively stealing from my children's education fund."**

Chapter 4
Investing with OPM

It was once explained to me that, as an investor, if you're not consistently prepared to conduct business with liquid capital readily available, you'll inevitably miss out on opportunities. I want to take a moment to emphasize the significance of finance.

The acronym **OPM** stands for "Other People's Money." It refers to borrowed capital used to amplify potential returns, a strategy employed by both individual investors and corporations. For new business owners and investors, this is a critical concept—but there's another essential rule: **never commingle funds.** I kept my personal accounts separate by housing them in a credit union, distinct from my business accounts. Novice investors often mix funds, which can severely impact cash flow and make it difficult to present clear business profits.

Building relationships with at least two banks is highly recommended for your business. This approach not only ensures you receive the necessary customer service but also positions you to play the OPM game effectively. It allows you to compare services and creates healthy competition between banks, which ultimately benefits your business.

Initially, my business account was solely with the large national bank BB&T, now known as Truist. However, I wanted to cultivate a relationship with a smaller local bank—one that made decisions with the community in mind.

Through an introduction, I met a prominent Chinese real estate investor in Virginia. He was courteous and agreed to introduce me to private lenders who specialized in helping people secure funding to launch businesses. He mentioned that I was being afforded this opportunity based on his reputation, as these lenders typically only assisted members of the Chinese community.

When I arrived at the meeting, I found myself in a luxurious setting, surrounded by conversations I couldn't understand, as everyone was speaking Mandarin. As a federal agent, I grasped the complexity of my situation and the potential implications of this meeting. I politely excused myself, asking the secretary if there was a restroom down the hall, but instead of returning, I went straight to my car. Later, I sent an email apologizing to the gentleman who had arranged the introduction, explaining that I didn't think it was the right fit for me.

Following that, I reached out to six local banks, aiming to speak with Vice Presidents of Commercial Lending or Loan Officers to arrange meetings. Five of the six banks were uninterested in working with a small investor managing properties between 9 and 12 units. However, one Vice President, DA from American Bank, expressed interest.

He agreed to meet with me briefly on his way home, provided I could accommodate his schedule. When I told him I worked in Falls Church, Virginia, he replied that it was convenient, as he lived nearby. He added, "Since my wife hasn't cooked, let's meet at the McDonald's just off I-66 near Falls Church. We can go over your portfolio over a burger."

Mr. DA gave me thirty minutes to discuss my resume, my story, and my business plan. During our meeting, he appeared genuinely engaged. He came across as a down-to-earth, middle-aged man who was giving me his full attention.

I had prepared copies of all the requested information, including a written summary of my story. During our meeting, I verbally briefed Mr. DA on the package I was leaving with him. It seemed he was genuinely impressed by my personable nature and by what I had accomplished in real estate in such a short span of time. He expressed considerable interest in my role as a Federal Agent and my background in Chicago. While DA initially indicated that he could only spare thirty minutes, we ended up staying at McDonald's, laughing and conversing for over an hour.

At the conclusion of our meeting, Mr. DA looked at me and asked, "Mr. Jenkins, what do you need from American Bank?"

I replied, "I believe having a solid relationship with a bank will lead to quicker decisions regarding my requests. I want a bank that feels like a partner each time I look to acquire real estate."

Specifically, I shared my desire for a line of credit to act swiftly on properties requiring substantial security deposits with offers. "Nobody can tell my story better than I can," I said. "I want to be able to call you and say, 'This is Vendarryl, and this is what I want to acquire,' and have you respond, 'Come, let's sit down and figure out how to make this deal happen.'"

I explained that, in my role as a Federal Agent, I always asked witnesses or victims at the end of an interview if there was anything pertinent I hadn't covered. More often than not, I received valuable information. I hoped to use the same approach when working with him on real estate deals. I noted that his knowledge of local ordinances or developments could influence my decisions. He smiled, instructed me to fill out a form, and said he'd run my credit scores while reviewing my package. He assured me he'd get back to me within a week.

Four days later, I received a call from Mr. DA's secretary to schedule a follow-up meeting at American Bank. When I arrived, Mr. DA greeted me with a smile and asked, "Vendarryl, are you ready to become a millionaire?"

He informed me that American Bank was eager to partner with me on my real estate journey. While acknowledging that I was still early in my journey and lacked certain experiences, he expressed his belief in my potential. He explained that he would establish parameters and guidelines since we would be partners in this process. He emphasized that my excellent credit scores opened significant opportunities for me.

Mr. DA also shared an important insight: every local bank has a board of directors that sets the bank's focus areas, and everything seemed to align for me to utilize OPM effectively. That day, he extended a $25,000 line of credit to me. In return, I opened an account at American Bank and began depositing the rental income from my property at 2501 Naylor Road.

The Importance of Credit Scores

Credit scores are one of the top three factors that can hinder someone from succeeding in real estate investing with OPM. Credit is a direct indicator to banks and creditors of one's reliability in paying bills and honoring commitments.

My credit was so important to me that I used to request quarterly printouts to monitor any fluctuations. This principle was instilled in both my wife and me by our parents: **pay your bills on time.**

Additionally, DA pointed out that my resume highlighted my thirteen years with the same job, which demonstrated stability. No bank wants to engage with someone who frequently jumps from job to job due to incompetence or behavioral issues.

One of Mr. DA's suggestions before we could proceed with a deal was to enlist an attorney to join my team. He explained that no reputable real estate management company could thrive without legal counsel in Washington, D.C. The District of Columbia is a tenant-friendly jurisdiction with numerous regulations designed to protect tenants' rights.

Washington, D.C., has intricate rent control laws that can easily land new landlords in significant trouble. I quickly realized Mr. DA was right, especially since I had been burned in D.C. court a few months earlier due to a technicality that cost me three months' rent.

I had been filing an eviction case and, after preparing the paperwork, decided to serve the tenant myself. The tenant enlisted the help of a law student from Howard University, who volunteered to assist low-income individuals in disputes with landlords. The technicality that derailed my case was that I had not served the paperwork in both Spanish and English, as required in D.C. The judge dismissed my case and ordered me to refile it, ensuring the tenant received notice in both languages.

While in court, I noticed an attorney representing several property management companies and landlords. After the hearing, I approached him, introduced myself as a landlord and property manager, and inquired about his services. His name was JA, and we arranged to meet shortly thereafter to discuss how he could assist me.

During our meeting, JA explained that all I needed to do was call him and send him the rent roll information. He would handle all my evictions with the court, ensuring compliance with D.C.'s complex legal requirements. Additionally, JA offered to advise me on corporate registrations as an LLC, business licenses, and Certificate of Occupancy issues.

Once you own properties with more than four units, you enter a different regulatory category and must navigate additional compliance requirements. JA emphasized the importance of having an attorney or accountant who can guide you in choosing the most suitable entity for your business endeavors.

When I purchased my first four-unit building, I initially operated as a sole proprietorship. I could have partnered with someone as either a general or limited partner, but I chose to go it alone. However, after consulting JA, I decided to establish LLCs for my properties. This legal structure separated each building, reducing the risk of a lawsuit jeopardizing all my real estate holdings. In today's litigious society, having an attorney on retainer is not just beneficial—it's essential.

In addition to hiring JA, I brought on an accountant to assist my wife with the financial aspects of our growing business. Andrew Hunt, an Alpha Phi Alpha Fraternity brother, specializes in accounting for real estate professionals. His expertise streamlined our bookkeeping processes and ensured our financial compliance.

These professional additions to my team enhanced my credibility as a landlord and investor. They signaled to banks, tenants, and partners alike that I was a serious and professional real estate investor, prepared to navigate the challenges of the industry.

Chapter 5
Favor ain't Fair

The philosophy that the greater the risk, the greater the potential gain applies to most investments, and real estate is no exception. I resolved to locate a distressed property in Washington, D.C., specifically in the Southeast area where my other holdings were located. Driving around the neighborhood, I occasionally noticed boarded-up buildings. I needed to figure out how to access information to determine if any of these properties were for sale. I explored foreclosures, MLS listings, and auctions—popular avenues for discovering various types of available buildings.

Most investors sought what are known as turnkey properties— buildings that are operational and already occupied by tenants. Sellers would extract all the equity, marketing these properties at a significant premium. There are several categories of properties you might encounter. One common type is mismanaged properties, where the owner struggles to keep up with repairs or tenant management and is eager to sell. These properties can often be purchased at a reasonable price, but you inherit all the seller's problems, putting you in an unenviable situation.

Another very profitable and sought-after type is a boarded-up building needing extensive repairs due to water damage, fire, roofing issues, or rodent infestation. If you can acquire this type of building at a low cost and address the damages, you have the potential for a highly valuable asset.

This was exactly the type of building I was hunting for at this stage of my journey. I likened it to hunting for Moby Dick—a massive undertaking, especially since I had narrowed my search to such a specific area. The process was often frustratingly difficult.

One Sunday afternoon, after church, I stopped by the grocery store to pick up something to cook for the kids. I rarely purchased the *Washington Post* because it was 2003, and most information was available online. For some reason, I noticed that this edition was marked as a "larger, classified edition." Intrigued, I picked up the paper, thumbed through it, and saw houses listed for sale. I decided to buy it and added it to my groceries.

When I got home, my wife and I cooked dinner together. Later, while sitting with the kids, my wife asked why I had purchased the *Washington Post*. I explained that I was planning to search the classifieds for another fixer-upper, ideally a 9-unit building.

When I finally found some time to browse the classified section, I came across an ad for a 9-unit building located at 4919 A Street SE, Washington, D.C., for sale by the owner. I quickly looked up the location and saw that it was near Benning Road and two streets off East Capitol Street.

I nearly fell out of my chair when I read the ad. It described exactly what I had been searching for—a property in need of "tender loving care" from a new owner. The ad invited interested parties to call for further details.

Excited, I glanced at the clock—it was 8:30 PM Eastern Time. Being in Virginia, I assumed it was too late to contact the seller. However, upon checking the phone number listed in the ad, I noticed it had a Los Angeles area code. It was only 5:30 PM Pacific Time. Realizing I still had a chance, I decided to make the call.

I spent a few moments contemplating what I would say before dialing the number. My extensive communication training gave me confidence in my ability to converse effectively. As a trained hostage negotiator and interview interrogator, I felt prepared for the conversation ahead.

When I called, I was greeted by the warm voice of what I suspected to be an older Black woman. Her friendly tone immediately put me at ease as I introduced myself formally.

"Ma'am," I began, "I am a real estate investor who specializes in properties that require some tender loving care. With your permission, I would like to arrange a time to view the building tomorrow. May I also inquire about the asking price?"

She responded that the price was negotiable and encouraged me to visit the property and make an offer.

We stayed on the phone for about an hour, talking not just about the building but also about Washington, D.C. She shared that she grew up in the building, which her mother had proudly purchased in 1965. "Wow," I said, "that's the year I was born—in Chicago." She chuckled at the coincidence and went on to tell me more about her life.

She had graduated from Howard University, married a man from Los Angeles, and moved to the West Coast after college, never to return to D.C. permanently. Her brother had been managing the property until he fell ill a few years ago, leading to the building's serious disrepair. She explained that she had visited the property a few months earlier and realized it would be best to sell it.

As we talked further, I began to understand the family dynamics that were troubling her. Her brother was terminally ill, and she did not want to co-own the building with his children, whom she barely knew. She described them bluntly as "a bunch of good-for-nothing drunks," though she emphasized that her relationship with her brother had always been good.

I empathized with her, sharing that I had children in an expensive private school. "I want to give them a first-class education," I said, "but I also want them to stay connected to their roots. They need to know where their Black people are, too. I'd have them come down on weekends to mop hallways, cut grass, and help clean up, so they understand where their tuition money comes from. If I can buy this building, it will leave a lasting impression on my kids—just like it did for you growing up."

She was impressed and said she admired my perspective.

The next day, I met with my heating and plumbing tradesmen, along with my electrician, at the property to inspect it. The building was partially boarded up, but to my surprise, three tenants were still living there. The roof had caved in on one side, causing significant water damage to part of the interior. However, the building's structure was sound, and most of the repairs were cosmetic.

After inspecting the property, I determined it would need a new roof, new windows, repaired walls, and new cabinets and subfloors in the water-damaged units.

That evening, I called the woman back, and we had another lengthy conversation. She informed me that, since our last discussion, she had spoken to about five other investors. They were highly motivated and had made substantial offers—without even visiting the property.

I reassured her that I had a strong relationship with a bank and could confidently close the deal within 60 days. I offered her $150,000 for the property. She acknowledged that my offer was lower than the others but said she would take it under consideration.

The following Tuesday morning, she called me again—this time in a state of panic. The building's heating system had malfunctioned, and the three tenants had reported the issue to the city. Given that it was winter, the apartments had become uncomfortably cold without heat.

She pleaded with me to meet the city inspector on her behalf and let her know what needed to be done to resolve the issue. I agreed, went to the building, and met with the inspector. He informed me that, at a minimum, two portable heating units would need to be purchased for each apartment until the main heating system could be repaired.

I emailed her a copy of the contract, and she signed it. At this point, I felt we were truly working together as a team. To address the heating issue, I went to Home Depot and purchased six portable heaters, which I delivered to the tenants. I also had my heating contractor assess the situation. It turned out that ordering parts for the thirty-year-old unit would take about a week.

Once the heating system was repaired and back in working order, I returned four of the portable heaters to Home Depot. I informed the seller that she owed me $700 for the heaters I had purchased for the tenants. True to her word, she mailed me the money, and I received it about six days later.

At this point, we were speaking about three times a week, and we had built a strong sense of trust. She even told the tenants that I was her nephew and that I would be taking over the building.

Purchasing a building and undertaking a total rehab was a risky endeavor, but I felt more confident than ever because of my solid relationship with American Bank. The bank had implemented checks and balances to ensure I followed through on my plans.

To streamline the process, I reached out to my cousin Girard, a construction engineer based in Chicago. I asked him to come to D.C. to draw up plans outlining the phases of the project. The construction funds would be disbursed in three installments as the work progressed.

The first disbursement covered the roof repairs and plumbing issues. The second installment was designated for installing new windows and strong security doors for both the front entrance and the individual apartments. The final draw would be used for cosmetic upgrades in each unit.

I had purchased the building for $150,000 and secured a consolidated construction loan for $120,000. Girard handled all the necessary paperwork to obtain the building permit. To meet local licensing requirements, I hired a "straw licensed contractor"—a term used in the construction industry for someone who provides their license number to sign off on documents and ensure the work is performed correctly.

When the contractor reviewed the package Girard had prepared, he remarked that my cousin clearly knew what he was doing, even though he lacked a D.C. license.

By this point, I had gathered all the documentation the bank required to close on the property and begin the project. At the closing, I was taken by surprise when the seller contributed $30,000 toward my closing costs. She explained that she wanted to support me in achieving the meaningful goals I had discussed for my family.

About two months after purchasing the building, the seller and I spoke to keep her updated on the progress of the rehab. During our conversation, she shared that her dear brother had passed away about 45 days after we closed the deal. I didn't have the heart to tell her that two of the female tenants had not paid rent for a very long time because her brother had been fooling around with them. He was an older man, and they had taken advantage of him.

I confronted the women and said, "Listen, you're both six months behind on rent. I'll give each of you $800 to leave within 30 days." They both agreed, took the money, and moved out as promised. This left me with two more vacant units to renovate. Once those units were fully renovated, I was able to charge about one-third more in rent than they had been paying—or were supposed to be paying.

Finally, I felt it was time to show the property to my wife, Shafonda. If she had seen the building in its original state—partially boarded up with a collapsing roof—she would have been horrified.

I felt guilty for not showing it to her earlier, but I couldn't risk it at the time. I was confident in my ability to make this project a success and was willing to shoulder that risk alone.

I brought her to see the building after the roof had been replaced and the new windows were being installed. Even then, she was visibly anxious. The building still required significant work before it could house tenants, and she worried about how we would manage the loan payments without rental income. I reassured her that since it was a construction loan, I was only responsible for paying the interest on the disbursed amounts. We had 90 days before the loan would be consolidated into a single mortgage.

During the final phase of construction, I developed a grueling routine. Every morning, I drove to Lowe's or Home Depot to stock my truck with supplies for the Hispanic crew working during the day. After putting in a full day at my federal agent job, I would stop by Home Depot in Capitol Heights to gather more materials for the night shift crew, who worked until midnight.

To protect my investment, I paid Mr. B to stay overnight in the building, armed, to prevent anyone from stealing supplies. This relentless schedule continued for nearly a month, leaving me physically and mentally drained.

Eventually, I had to fly out of town for work, utterly exhausted from the pressure of getting 4919 A Street SE ready for tenants. Though I was close to the finish line, the stress was taking a toll. During the flight, the attendant offered me a drink, and as I lifted it to my mouth, it spilled down my shirt. A wave of fear swept over me—I thought I might be having a stroke.

I stood up to go to the restroom and noticed that the left side of my face had started to droop. When I arrived at the hotel and met my co-workers, they immediately said, "Call 911—he's had a stroke."

The next thing I knew, I was being whisked away in an ambulance to the hospital as a stroke victim.

What the old folks say is true: when you think you're in an emergency, you start calling on God. As I lay there, I began singing Mary Mary's song in my head:

"I just can't give up now. I've come too far from where I started from. Nobody told me the road would be easy, and I don't believe He's brought me this far to leave me."

When I arrived at the hospital, the doctors ran a battery of tests and determined that I had a condition called Bell's Palsy. My immune system was severely weakened from overworking, which led to an infection in my throat. The infection pinched a nerve, causing the left side of my face to shut down. Fortunately, it wasn't a stroke, and I was sent home with an escort to rest and follow up with my doctor back home.

At this point, the building was 90% complete, and I couldn't afford to slow down for long. I took two days off to recover, then got back to work to finish the project. We were only two weeks away from the loan being consolidated, and I knew I couldn't let the building sit vacant while I started paying the mortgage. I dreaded how my wife would react if we had to dip into other accounts to cover the mortgage for more than a month.

I leaned heavily on my contacts within social agencies that my mentor had introduced me to, and I managed to fill the units quickly. One of the key lessons I learned from this experience was the importance of balance. While I could have filled the entire building with fully subsidized Section 8 tenants, I recognized the value of maintaining a mix.

By keeping half the units occupied by working tenants paying reduced rates, I ensured there were people in the building who could serve as my eyes and ears. These tenants would report disturbances—like fights or loud music—that Section 8 tenants were less likely to report, as they were often participants in the chaos themselves. Filling the building entirely with subsidized tenants might have temporarily boosted cash flow, but it would have compromised the building's long-term stability.

God's favor was evident throughout this ordeal. Within 120 days, I had fully renovated the building and filled it with tenants. This became my greatest real estate achievement. Once the building was fully operational and generating premium rents, its value had more than doubled, increasing my net worth by $270,000 on paper in a very short period.

To top it off, my face gradually returned to normal over the next three weeks.

Everything fell into place at 4919 A Street SE. Though I had pushed myself to the brink of exhaustion, I ultimately succeeded. *Favor ain't fair!*

Chapter 6
Paper Millionaire

After four years of being a landlord and managing two dozen units, I developed an efficient system for all my properties. I converted a bottom unit in my A Street property into an administrative office and supply area. My new system standardized everything—paint, cabinets, carpet, kitchen and bathroom hardware, smoke detectors, and ceiling fans were the same across all units. My goal was to replicate the McDonald's principle: consistency in quality and appearance.

When a unit became vacant, it was straightforward to turn it around within ten days because the materials were always on hand, and my maintenance staff was familiar with the layout. However, I learned that no unit is truly ready until someone moves in. As a rule, before a new tenant occupied a unit, I would spend an entire day in it, even showering there, to ensure everything was in working order. I believed that if a unit was good enough for me, it would be good enough for a prospective renter.

I aimed to continue expanding my real estate portfolio, but the question loomed: what would I do next? Several viable opportunities within my price range presented themselves.

The first opportunity was to join an investment fund. A professional fund manager was meeting with investors to raise $5 million for the purchase of a large property. Each investor would contribute $100,000, with an expected return of 8–10%. This passive investment opportunity appealed to me because it would allow me to generate income without taking on the management responsibilities of more tenants. Additionally, it would diversify my portfolio with a different class of property.

Another option came from my real estate social network, where I met silent investors interested in partnering with me. They wanted to make me a general partner in properties they invested in, with me handling all day-to-day operations. While this was an exciting prospect, I had to weigh the responsibilities and risks. As a general partner, I would share profits but also take on unlimited liability—a significant consideration.

Meanwhile, my real estate connections in Southeast D.C. alerted me to another opportunity: a nine-unit building located at 5036 Astor Place was about to hit the market. This building was only two blocks away from my previous purchase at 4919 A Street, and I couldn't resist its potential. It felt like a sign from God.

I quickly withdrew my interest in the other opportunities, such as becoming a general partner or joining an investment fund, and focused my energy on the Astor Place property. However, the seller, realizing how significant this investment was to me given its proximity to my other properties, adopted a hardball approach during negotiations.

Typically, I excel at negotiating favorable deals in a buyer's market. My strategy involves securing the property under contract and using the due diligence stage to negotiate the price down based on any findings. Unfortunately, this negotiation took a different turn. The seller demanded an unreasonable 10% deposit upfront with my offer, which immediately made me uneasy.

To make matters worse, the investor who informed me about the building also shared sensitive information about me with the seller. This betrayal complicated the process and added tension to the negotiations.

In retrospect, I let my emotions get the best of me with the Astor Place building because it was so close to my other property. I became fixated on adding it to my portfolio, feeling like I had to have it. However, the current rents in the building were low, and I would be facing numerous rent control challenges. Rent control is a city government system designed to limit the rate at which a landlord can increase a tenant's rent.

I eventually got the building under contract, but I made concessions I would have walked away from in any other deal. Normally, I avoid becoming emotionally attached to a property because it makes you lose your negotiating edge. In real estate investing, the profit is often made at the price point you negotiate upfront. When properties fall into mismanagement or physical decay, they typically come with the expectation of a significant discount.

This building had substantial tenant issues that the owner was unwilling to address, which had motivated him to sell. Knowing this, I should have delayed and pushed harder for better terms. The property's potential value was around $400,000 with top rents, assuming the tenant issues were resolved. I offered $290,000 for the property, but my goal had been to pay closer to $200,000. I estimated it would take about three years to resolve the tenant problems and elevate the cash flow to reflect the property's true value.

During the financing stage, I determined that the best option for acquiring this property was a wraparound mortgage that included another property. I leveraged the equity from 4919 A Street as collateral, consolidating both properties under a single mortgage loan.

While the bank was conducting its financial evaluations, the Vice President of the bank invited me in for a meeting. When I arrived, he started a conversation about the growth of my net worth. He explained that by calculating my liabilities and subtracting them from my total assets and bank balances, he had determined that, in just four years, I had acquired three buildings and three houses, all with substantial equity.

He said, "I'm happy to tell you that your net worth is over a million dollars. You're what we call a paper millionaire, Mr. Jenkins."

I responded, "Well, now I can pay full tuition for my kids and buy a house for my parents to help them out—all thanks to real estate. But honestly, I don't feel like a millionaire. In fact, I don't feel much different at all."

He smiled and said, "Wealth often grows incrementally, like a kid's growth spurt. Every year, I measured my kids' growth by marking their height on a wall. They were always so surprised when they saw the difference from the previous year. It's the same with your finances—you're taking care of business for your family, and now you're in a great financial position."

Even though I explained what the VP said to my wife—an accountant with an MBA—she wasn't impressed. She just said, "Boy, you're not a real millionaire. Go sit down somewhere."

My wife, ever the chef serving up humble pies, ensured I kept a healthy dose of humility.

8582 Adamson Street property

5352 Hayes ST. Property

After closing on 5036 Astor Place SE, I encountered the most contemptuous tenants I had ever faced in my journey as a landlord. I personally visited each unit to introduce myself, only to discover that more than half of the tenants were immediately hostile. Many threatened legal action or declared their intention to withhold rent. It quickly became evident that these tenants believed the sale process had been improperly conducted, claiming they had been deprived of their right to come together and purchase the building themselves.

Under Washington, D.C. law, tenants must be given a designated period to secure funding and exercise their right of first refusal to purchase a property being sold. The tenants alleged that the seller had not afforded them this opportunity. Typically, sellers attempt to navigate this process by meeting with tenants and having them sign a form indicating they do not wish to purchase the building.

In an effort to resolve the situation, I tried to engage with the tenants directly, but some of their behaviors were outright appalling.

The tenants retained an attorney, forcing me to incur significant legal fees to defend myself, despite the fact that I had not been involved in the seller's alleged actions. This became an expensive and frustrating ordeal. Ultimately, however, the tenants lacked both the financial resources and the unity among themselves to move forward with purchasing the property.

To complicate matters, they were also not paying their rent. Once they lost in the legal proceedings, they vacated the premises without fulfilling their financial obligations. While I was relieved to have the situation resolved, the process was costly and served as a harsh reminder of the challenges of dealing with tenant disputes.

The building on Astor Place was the first property in my portfolio where I had to evict multiple tenants simultaneously. Being forced to go to court for four months over rent collections resulted in significant financial losses. One of the most memorable eviction cases during this period involved a single mother with three children who had fallen behind on her rent. She explained that her employment had been disrupted because one of her children was frequently ill.

While I felt deep compassion for her circumstances, I also recognized that every real estate investor must decide whether to operate as a social service provider or as a businessperson. After several months of nonpayment, I reluctantly initiated eviction proceedings against her, and the court granted the order.

In Washington, D.C., it is customary to hire the U.S. Marshals to carry out evictions. On the day of the eviction, the mother was in the middle of preparing a meal for her children, who were seated at the table eagerly awaiting their food. The Marshals informed her that she needed to vacate the unit immediately and could not finish feeding her children.

The scene tugged at my heart. I asked the Marshals if they could allow the children to eat before leaving, but they firmly stated that if I slowed them down, they would leave entirely, as they had five more evictions scheduled that day.

Feeling helpless, I quickly got into my car and drove to McDonald's, where I bought three Happy Meals for the children. When I returned to the unit, I apologized to the mother for the timing of the eviction and assured her that I would never stand by and allow children to go hungry in such a situation. I handed her the food and said, "Please feed your children."

To my shock, she cursed at me, snatched the bag, and dumped the food onto the ground. Her children screamed and cried, "Mommy, we're hungry!" She ordered them to get into the car and wait for her.

Stunned and upset by her actions, I quickly got back in my truck and drove away. That day left a lasting impression on me—not only because of her behavior but also because of the emotional weight of the eviction process.

The Astor Place property continued to present challenges for over a year before I was finally able to manage it effectively and achieve consistent rental income. I've learned that most properties will have, at a minimum, about 20% problem tenants. However, Astor Place had three times that number, making it an exceptionally difficult experience.

Looking back, I can honestly say I'm not sure I would have survived the journey had this been my first property.

Chapter 7
The 80 percent

Any type of residential real estate property you acquire will inevitably include approximately 20% of tenants who are problematic—troublemakers, non-rent payers, or otherwise difficult to manage. These individuals are often tenants you inherited when purchasing the building or, occasionally, those you misjudged and gave keys to yourself.

This book, along with other resources on being a landlord, will delve extensively into how to handle such tenants. Problematic renters are often the primary reason many investors shy away from managing their own properties. Whenever I mention that I manage my own buildings to maintain direct oversight in real time, people often react negatively, sharing horror stories they've heard about renters.

I proudly explain that, when I first got married, my wife and I rented a small one-bedroom apartment while we saved to buy a house. In fact, for half my childhood, my family and I were renters ourselves—a fact I share without hesitation.

That said, I want to dedicate a chapter to discussing the majority of renters—the 80% of decent tenants you will encounter as a landlord.

At a back-to-school night at my kids' school, I recall a teacher explaining how she managed an overcrowded public school classroom. She shared that, in every class, about 25% of students were below grade level. She did her best for them with limited time and resources. Another 15% were above average in various ways, but time constraints often prevented her from giving them as much attention as they deserved. They often became her helpers or peer tutors.

Her focus, she explained, was primarily on the 60% of students who fell in the middle. These were the students who made the most progress with her guidance and demanded the bulk of her time and effort.

This approach is strikingly similar to managing tenants as a landlord. Just as classrooms have high-achievers, strugglers, and the majority in the middle, so do rental properties.

The largest segment of tenants falls in the middle—a mix of decent renters who occasionally require attention for minor issues. Preparing a unit for a new tenant costs at least $1,000, so it's in every landlord's best interest to develop tolerance and a clear understanding of what behaviors you're willing to accept. Success as a landlord hinges on keeping rent rolls up and maintenance costs down while managing tenants effectively.

When dealing with tenants from lower socioeconomic backgrounds, minor issues involving drugs or alcohol are common. For example, in Washington, D.C., marijuana use is legal, and some tenants use it frequently. However, other tenants may be intolerant of the smell, creating the need for negotiation to maintain peace.

Though I don't smoke marijuana myself, I researched ways to address the issue. I suggested using incense, rolling a towel at the front door, closing vents, or switching to vaping. The tenant, who always paid rent on time and was generally respectful, agreed to these adjustments. I explained, "You live in this building with eight other families, so I need you to be respectful." The matter was resolved diplomatically.

Alcohol-related issues were another recurring challenge, particularly on weekends. Alcohol sometimes led to domestic disputes or conflicts between tenants.

One notable incident involved two otherwise responsible tenants—hardworking individuals who paid rent on time and followed the rules. One Saturday night, two couples were drinking and playing cards, which led to an argument over the game's rules. The conflict escalated as unrelated grievances surfaced, including accusations about food borrowing. Finally, one person questioned the paternity of the other's youngest child.

When I arrived, I found blood in the hallway and two holes in the living room wall. Although I was furious, I chose not to overreact. Instead, I billed both tenants for the damages and counseled them sternly. I warned that any future incidents would result in eviction.

To be transparent, minor alcohol-related issues like this occurred about once a year. Managing these situations effectively required a combination of firmness, fairness, and diplomacy.

Consistent late payment of rent was a common issue among the 60% of tenants who were generally decent but not without their challenges. My perspective on this came from an experience I had as a young Air Force airman. In the military, the workday started at

7:30 a.m., and I would sit in my car until precisely 7:30 before walking into the building.

One day, a strict new sergeant took over our shop. During a meeting, he emphasized that tardiness would not be tolerated. A few days later, he called me into his office and said, "Airman Jenkins, despite my warning, you're still arriving late." I was confused and explained that I was arriving at exactly 7:30. He replied, "Arriving at 7:30 is not *before* 7:30—it's *after*. I've tracked your times for the past month, and you've consistently arrived three to four minutes late."

I was stunned, thinking he was being unnecessarily strict. But then he explained, "There are twenty other people in this section who make the effort to arrive five minutes early to ensure they aren't late. I wake up early, get my kids dressed, pack their lunches, drop them off, and still arrive on time. If I let you continue showing up late, even by a few minutes, what message does that send?" He added firmly, "If you're late again—by any amount of time—I'll send you to corrective custody for 90 days."

His words hit home, and from that point forward, I made sure to arrive at 7:25 a.m. every day.

As a landlord, I didn't have the authority to impose corrective custody on tenants, but I could share that story. When tenants failed to pay rent by the fifth of the month, I would tell them, "I have to charge you a late fee, or what message am I sending to those who pay on time?" Of course, I made exceptions in certain cases and waived late fees when circumstances warranted it.

For tenants who consistently paid late but managed to settle by the tenth, I reluctantly tolerated it. To encourage timely payments, I occasionally offered incentives, such as waiving the twelfth month's rent for tenants who paid on time for eleven consecutive months. Ironically, no one ever managed to win that reward, despite how simple it seemed.

Adult relationships naturally developed in the close quarters of the buildings, but problems arose when those relationships ended, often leaving hurt feelings and drama that affected other tenants. Things got particularly messy when one or both parties involved were married, leading to tensions that spilled over into the building. On a few occasions, I had to involve the police due to acts of vandalism.

Ensuring the building was a safe space for everyone, including members of the LGBTQ+ community, was always a priority. One of my favorite tenants was a lesbian named DT, who worked in law enforcement. She proudly displayed her firearm qualification targets in her apartment, and when I showed her one of mine—a perfect 100—she liked it so much she hung it up alongside hers.

DT lived in the basement, next to the boiler room. One day, she asked, "Mr. Jenkins, are you going to be around in about an hour?" Suspicious, I asked why. DT replied with a smirk, "I've got a bad married redbone woman coming through at 4 p.m., and I want you to see her." Laughing, I said, "DT, I'm not getting involved in your mess with these married women."

When I finished my work in the boiler room, it was ten minutes to 4 p.m., so I sat on the basement steps, curious. Sure enough, DT walked in with a tall, beautiful woman. She introduced me to her "friend" with a wink and a smug look that said, "I told you so." I laughed, slapped her hand, and left the building.

Not all tenants were as entertaining as DT. One tenant who gave me constant trouble was a six-foot-two trans woman who frequently got into fights. Anyone assuming her femininity meant weakness learned otherwise quickly. She was always brawling, whether on the block or inside the building. When I tried to address it with her, she'd always say, "Mr. Jenkins, they keep messing with me, sir!"

Other tenants pushed boundaries in smaller ways, like sneaking in large pets, allowing unauthorized occupants, or leaving the front security door propped open. In one building, I spent a significant amount of money installing a steel security door to prevent intruders from sneaking into the laundry room to sleep. When I began locking the laundry room at night, tenants complained.

Despite the investment in security, some tenants repeatedly left the door propped open for guests without keys, undermining the very safety measures they had requested. These infractions were frustrating but, unfortunately, part of the job.

A common trend I noticed was adult children moving back in with their parents for a "reset." This wasn't unique to my buildings—it seemed to be happening everywhere, even in my own family. What was supposed to be a three-month stay often stretched into a year or more.

One situation I was particularly strict about was when a tenant housed someone on house arrest. One of my best tenants called and asked if her son could stay with her if he got out of jail with an ankle monitor. "Please, Mr. Jenkins, this is my child," she pleaded. I agreed to consider it but asked to see his paperwork. When I discovered he had been jailed for a violent rape, I told her he could stay for only 60 days while he found a suitable place. "He may be your baby," I explained, "but I have female tenants with young daughters, and they won't feel comfortable." I also made it clear that I would inform the other tenants.

She was furious, and ultimately, he stayed for only a month—especially after insisting on bringing a massive pit bull into the building.

Fifteen percent of my tenants were the kind you dream of: they paid their rent on time, followed all the rules, and rarely contacted me. Mrs. Maddie and Hermon were in that category. Initially grumpy, they eventually warmed up to me and wanted me to visit often for a chat. On Saturdays, I set aside 20 minutes to sit and have tea with them. The only issue was that their unit was incredibly cluttered, and they kept heaters running year-round because they were always cold.

Mr. G was another favorite tenant—an elderly man who came with the building when I bought it. In his seventies, he had a girlfriend in her thirties and her young son. I'll never forget how the boy looked at me one day and said, "You're a Black man, and you own this building?"

"Yes," I replied, "and when you grow up, you can own a building too."

He grinned and said, "I'm going to do that, Mr. Jenkins—you watch."

Mr. G worked long shifts and was often tired, but he loved to joke that his young girlfriend "kept his battery charged." He'd say, "When she reaches over and touches me early in the morning, my battery charges up like I'm a young man again." I laughed and said, "Mr. G, she's keeping you young—keep it up!"

One evening, I was at the building and saw Mr. G coming home from work, looking completely worn out. I smiled and said, "Mr. G, get yourself a hot bath and a bite to eat, and get that battery charged up—you'll be like brand new."

He smiled back and said, "That's exactly what I'm going to do, Mr. Jenkins." We both chuckled and went about our evening.

There's a verse from Rudyard Kipling's poem *"If"* that reads: *"If you can talk with crowds and keep your virtue, or walk with kings—but not lose the common touch."* To me, that means having the social fluidity to make both kings and everyday people feel at ease in your company.

A good friend once invited my wife and me to a jazz concert at the White House. We went through all the expected security and gave our names. To our surprise, we were escorted to the second row, right at the front of the room.

As the seating filled up, I noticed two empty seats directly in front of us. A few minutes later, they announced, "Please rise for the President of the United States, George W. Bush, and First Lady Laura Bush."

To my amazement, the President and First Lady sat directly in front of us. During the concert, President Bush leaned back a few times, tapped my leg, and said, "I love this music," grinning widely. It was a surreal experience—and, to my surprise, it was televised for the world to see.

The next day, I went to one of my buildings to pay some workers and check on things. Mrs. Williams, one of my favorite tenants, was hosting a birthday party in the parking lot—against the rules, but I let it slide. They were grilling, playing go-go music, and dancing.

"Mr. Jenkins, come get something to eat!" they called out. I waved them off, but they insisted. I sat down for a burger and a Coke.

"Stay, Mr. Jenkins, we're about to cut the cake," they said. I stayed, and after singing "Happy Birthday," while eating my slice of cake, one tenant said, "Mr. Jenkins was on TV with the President of the United States yesterday, and today he's here with us in a parking lot in Southeast D.C."

Another chimed in, "We saw you, Mr. Jenkins!"

I smiled at the surreal contrast and said, "What can I say? I live an extraordinary life." I raised my can of Coke and added, "Cheers."

While this book will mostly discuss the worst situations and the most challenging tenants—the D and F tenants—it wouldn't be fair if I didn't take a moment to acknowledge the A, B, and C tenants who brought joy, meaning, and balance to my journey as a landlord.

Chapter 8
Provision

"Honor your father and your mother, so that you may live long in the land the Lord your God is giving you." *(Exodus 20:12)*

After purchasing three nine-unit buildings, a four-unit building, and two rental houses, my wife and I managed a total of 33 units. The cash flow from these properties provided us with significant financial stability. We were able to invest, save, and take family trips—all funded by this income.

One of the smartest investments we made was purchasing 529 educational investment plans for our kids. We locked in five years of tuition at current rates for any Virginia state-run school. This was invaluable in setting our children up for success.

God also provided me with the means to help my parents when they needed it the most—a blessing I will forever be grateful for.

During one of my visits to Chicago, I stayed at my parents' house in Dixmoor. I was in the back room watching TV while my mom cooked dinner. She accidentally dozed off, and something on the stove began to smoke. The fire alarm blared, filling the house with smoke. I ran to the kitchen to address the situation, but it was still quite smoky.

"Momma, open the door to get some air in here and clear out this smoke," I said.

That's when I noticed the bars on the windows, the iron security door, and the multiple locks requiring keys to open from both inside and outside.

"Lord, where are those keys?" my mother exclaimed, frantically searching. "I just had them on the counter!"

I watched her fumble around for two or three minutes before finally finding the keys and unlocking the three locks.

"Why do you have so many locks on the doors?" I asked. "This feels like a jail. If there had been an actual fire and you were disoriented, you could've been trapped. This is a fire hazard!"

She sighed deeply and replied, "Well, baby, it's just your daddy and me here, and folks are breaking in and killing people. You know how crazy this town gets around the holidays."

Later, as we talked, my mom asked about the new house Shafonda and I had just built in Virginia.

"Momma gets so happy thinking about my baby living in a new construction house," she said. "I know I'll never live in anything like that, but just knowing you do makes me happy."

I looked at her and said, "You never know, Momma. Your baby boy might build you a house one day."

She shook her head with a small smile. "Boy, hush. You've got those kids to raise and get through college."

Her words reminded me of the stories I'd heard from athletes who made it big, talking about how proud they were to buy their moms a house.

When my father came home that evening from working at the tire business he had built and named after his first grandson, **VJ Tire Center**, I could see his body was beginning to break down. Diabetes, arthritis, and stress were taking their toll.

My dad had forged a successful business in one of the toughest parts of Chicago—the Bronzeville neighborhood—just two blocks away from the notorious Robert Taylor Housing Projects. Over the years, he had contracts with the Chicago White Sox, the Chicago Housing Authority, Yellow Cab, and countless other steady clients.

But no matter how strong your work ethic, if your team of professionals drops the ball, trouble can follow. My father had fallen into serious issues with city sales taxes. They began charging him interest on unpaid back taxes, and the mounting debt put his 30 years of hard work in jeopardy.

Seeing this, I went back home and talked to my wife. I told her, "I believe God has helped me in excess because He's making provision for what's about to happen."

I began searching for a house for my parents and found a new construction development. Without telling them, I put down a deposit on a lot and made plans to start construction.

Meanwhile, back in Chicago, things were worsening with my father's tax situation, and the stress was becoming unbearable for him.

I knew my father was a proud man, and I couldn't simply say, "I'm buying you a house." Instead, I framed it as a real estate investment opportunity. At the time, in Virginia, new construction homes in early development phases often appreciated significantly within a year. Many investors would buy during the first phase and sell quickly to capitalize on the increase in value.

I explained my plan to him: "There's a new development, and it's a bit far out," I said. "I got some information from a realtor that, in ten years, property in that area will really appreciate. I want to buy a house there, but I need your help. I'd like you and Momma to live in the house and take care of it for me while it appreciates in value."

He responded, "I appreciate the opportunity, and thanks for thinking about us, but no thanks."

Despite his refusal, I felt strongly that God was guiding me to move forward with the construction and financing of the house.

Later, when my parents came to visit us in Virginia, I took them out to see the new house. Even then, my father remained adamant that he wasn't interested in leaving Chicago. Acting on faith, I pressed forward with the project, determined to help them despite his reluctance.

About a month later, the IRS took aggressive action against my father, threatening to shut down his tire business. His financial situation had reached a breaking point. I said, "Dad, I can help you if you move to Virginia. I'll put everything in my name so you can continue to live."

Reluctantly, he agreed to leave Chicago and move into the home I had prepared for them months earlier.

God had shown me favor and abundance—what I call "provision"—and I realized my journey wasn't just about me or the financial blessings we had received. God was using me as a vessel to provide for my parents in their time of need.

My wife and I have never been selfish people. We were blessed to have great government jobs and steady cash flow from the 33 units we owned and managed, which allowed us to extend that blessing to my parents.

We hurried to Chicago, packed up my parents, and brought them to stay with us in Virginia for about a month while the house was finalized.

When the house was ready, my wife and I handed them the keys to their newly constructed home. The joy we felt was immeasurable. I told them, "You'll never have to worry about a house payment again in your life."

At that moment, I realized you don't need to be a one-in-a-million entertainer or athlete to buy your parents a house. I had done it, and it was one of the greatest accomplishments of my life.

Three years had passed since I became a landlord, and I had grown accustomed to people calling me "Mr. Jenkins" out of respect. It was a status thing, a subtle acknowledgment of the landlord-tenant relationship. When I pulled up to the buildings in my unmistakable red pickup truck, there was always a vibe from the tenants: I was a cool guy—but not *that* cool.

When my dad moved to town, he naturally wanted to get involved in the real estate and help me manage the tenants. His presence filled a void I didn't even realize was there—it reminded me of how much I missed my cousin Spencer. Having my dad around brought a new energy to the buildings, but it also created a minor dilemma for the tenants. Since I was already "Mr. Jenkins," they had to come up with something for him. To my mild annoyance, they settled on "Big Mr. Jenkins" for him and "Little Mr. Jenkins" for me.

At first, I didn't love it, but since every tenant across all the buildings picked it up, I decided to just roll with it. My dad was clearly in his element. When we were together, it was obvious he still thought he was in charge, even though this was my operation. He fit right in with the team, doing a great deal of painting and repairs. Working alongside me helped him move past the tax issues and the loss of his tire business in Chicago.

The tenants loved watching us work together, often commenting that we were like a comedy act. One day, while we were installing a base cabinet under the kitchen sink, we bickered like father and son about how to remove the old cabinet and install the new one. The back of the cabinet had perforated lines showing where to cut it. My dad insisted we didn't need to cut all the way along the lines because he had measured it.

I said, "Dad, if the manufacturer put perforated lines there, they're telling you where to cut."

He responded, "Listen, I'm your father, and this is what we're going to do."

I relented. "Okay, let's do it your way."

We put the cabinet in, and—of course—it didn't fit. The entire perforated portion needed to be cut out.

He sighed. "Damn, you were right."

"Yup," I said with a grin. "Let's take it out and cut it properly." Then I joked, "From now on, I'm your daddy."

The tenants overheard our exchange and burst out laughing. They thought it was the funniest thing and said we were better than a sitcom. These moments happened almost weekly when we worked together.

Ensuring my parents were settled and happy was incredibly important to me, especially my mother, who had always been my rock. Like most mothers, her greatest wish was for her son to be happy.

There's one memory from my childhood that still permeates my mind and soul. When I was in sixth grade, I tried out for the Lincoln Wildcats basketball team. I had worked hard over the summer, and it paid off—I made the team and was even part of the starting five for the season opener.

Coach Sanders announced, "The team colors are green and gold, so your parents need to buy green Converse All-Star gym shoes and a green sweatsuit to match."

I knew money was tight at home, so I waited to tell my parents until they were both together. When I did, my father said, "You can only get one of the two, so you choose."

I replied, "Obviously, I need the gym shoes to play the game, but I want the sweatsuit, too."

He said, "You've made my point for me. My job is to get you what you need, not what you want." Then he got up from the table to take his bath and prepare for bed.

I ran to my mother and pleaded, "Momma, you've got to figure out a way to get that sweatsuit!"

She sighed. "Your father said no, and we just don't have the money. Let it go, baby."

That night, I prayed over and over for God to intervene.

The next morning, as my father left for work, I went to my mom's room and asked again. She just looked at me with sadness in her eyes and said, "He said no."

I broke down crying. To an eleven-year-old, this felt like the end of the world. I begged, "Momma, please figure out a way— before two o'clock."

By lunch, the school was buzzing with excitement for the first game and the pep rally. All the boys were showing off their new sweatsuits, and someone asked, "Vendarryl, where's your sweatsuit?"

"My mom's bringing it before the pep rally," I lied.

At 1:00 p.m., we went to the bathroom to change into our uniforms. My mother still hadn't shown up. I started praying even harder.

At 1:40 p.m., Coach Sanders came in to gather us for the pep rally, and my mom still wasn't there. I got up, head hanging, ready to join the team when someone shouted, "Vendarryl, is that your mom with your sweatsuit?"

I thought they were clowning me until I turned around and saw my mom walking toward the school with a J.C. Penney bag in her hand.

I sprinted out of the classroom, nearly knocking her over as I hugged her. She handed me the bag and said, "Won't God do it?"

She explained, "I told a lady I work with about your situation, and she pulled money out of her purse and said, 'Hurry to the store and get it for him.'"

That moment taught me the power of faith, kindness, and the sacrifices our mothers make for us.

My faith in God grew so much that day because I knew it was nothing but God's mercy, and he had heard my eleven-year-old cries. I went to the pep rally and enjoyed all the school spirit for the game. My mother stayed for the game, and I scored my first three points in my basketball career—a free throw and a rebound put-back.

In Chapter Two, I briefly mentioned how a sixteen-year-old boy knocked me out cold when I was twelve. The aftermath of that incident profoundly changed the way I perceived my father and ignited a desire within me to emulate him.

My lip was in bad shape, swollen from the blunt force trauma inflicted by the boy's fist. When my dad arrived home from work around 8 p.m., it was already dusk. My mother was crying, exclaiming, "Look what that monster did to my baby's face!"

My father glanced at me and calmly asked, "How old is this guy?"

I replied, "Dad, he's sixteen, and he goes to the high school."

Without another word, my father turned and went into his bedroom. I saw him rummaging through a shoebox and retrieving his revolver. He declared, "This is criminal, and I can't let this happen to my son."

He looked at me and said, "Son, put your jacket on. We're going to this boy's house tonight, and something is going to happen."

My mother grew frantic and tried to stop him. "No, Bobby, you could get killed going to those people's house at this hour!" she pleaded.

My father didn't waver. As we walked out the door, he told me, "Son, sometimes you must stand up for yourself, no matter the danger."

When we arrived at the boy's house, his father answered the door and sternly asked, "What can I do for you at this hour?"

My father responded, "I'm sorry to come to your home so late, but there's been a serious incident caused by your son."

He moved me to the front and said, "This is my twelve-year-old son, and your sixteen-year-old son did this to his face."

The man's expression softened as he invited us in. "Please, come in. Let's get to the bottom of this."

We sat down at the kitchen table. My father placed his revolver on the table, making his intentions clear. "Sir, my son was hurt and disfigured today by your son."

The man remained calm and turned to me. "Young man, why would my son hit you like this?"

I explained, "I was walking a girl from my class home from school, and he came up and told me to leave because he was going home with her. She begged me not to leave her because your son was harassing her."

The father frowned. "How old is this little girl?"

"She's twelve years old, just like me," I replied.

The man's demeanor shifted. He called for his son to come into the kitchen immediately. At the same time, he opened a closet and pulled out an extension cord.

When the boy arrived, his father asked him directly, "Did you do this to this boy's face?"

The boy hesitated but finally admitted, "Yes, sir. I hit him because he wouldn't leave when I told him to."

His father's anger was palpable. "The girl is only twelve years old!" he shouted. He told his son to strip down to his underclothes and then whipped him severely with the extension cord, all while repeating, "She's only twelve years old!"

By the time he was done, the sixteen-year-old was on the floor, whimpering and crying. The man, still breathing heavily, turned to my father and asked, "Are you good?"

My father picked up his revolver, placed it back in his pocket, and replied, "There's nothing more to say or do on this matter."

We left the house and returned home. My dad sat down to eat his dinner while I sat at the table, trying to process everything that had just happened.

As a twelve-year-old, I struggled to fully grasp the gravity of that night. Only as an adult did I come to understand the many ways it could have gone horribly wrong.

"I was young, and now I am old, yet I have never seen the righteous forsaken or their children begging for bread." (Psalms 37:25)

Chapter 9
Splitting Time

The first time I set a long-term plan was to endeavor to get money for my college education with veterans' benefits. I joined the Air Force less than a month after graduating high school to get the GI Bill to pay for my college education. When I honorably finished my enlistment, I started college at Chicago State University. I remember one Saturday morning I was spending some time at the epicenter of black culture—the barber shop. Things usually got really rowdy at that barber shop down on 47th Street in the hood. Every other Saturday morning, I was there like clockwork.

This particular Saturday, one of the older customers was in the barber shop, talking loudly and holding court about how stupid the younger generation was. He was a tall, dark guy with glasses who was walking around, talking crazy to everybody. He said, "I am going to ask one specific question, and you will see how silly these young boys are." He asked, "If you could request one thing in your life to have in abundance, what would it be?" "One guy shouted out, 'I want more money, and in abundance greater than I could ever spend!'" "Another guy shouted out, 'I want more sex; I want two or three women in bed with me!'" The barbershop erupted, going up several octaves in sound with screams and laughter.

At some point, I knew he was going to get to me after he strolled through all the young patrons waiting for haircuts. I happened to be already sitting in the barber's chair, getting my favorite haircut called "Fade to Black." That haircut was a high-top fade, neatly tapered and faded all the way down to the bald skin. The older guy turned and looked at me and said, "What do you have to say, college boy? What do you want in abundance?" I pondered for a moment and replied, "I would like to have an abundance of time; I never have enough of it." I was always stressed out over time as a whole. Time made me feel like a fat, hungry kid who hardly had enough food to eat.

He looked shocked and asked me, "How old are you, college boy?" I told him that I was twenty-three and working a full-time job while going to college full-time, taking four classes a semester and two in the summer. The older guy said, "Son, you are ahead of your time. Usually, people don't find out that until they are forty." Some days, I literally would leave work and go to class, then go to the library until midnight and start the whole thing over again. The thought that kept me going was the hope that one day my life would be different and that I would have more time once I started a career. It never changed for me, and I expanded to managing my time and teaching other people about the importance of time.

As a landlord it is your responsibility to create a system that impresses upon tenants that it is important to pay their rent every month timely. Rent is customarily paid at the first of the month with a few days grace period. In smaller residential buildings in low-income areas, you are generally working with people with marginal credit scores that you need to manage. A landlord should be creative to get out in front of these tenants with bad habits of paying rent whenever they can. One of the reasons that rents should be set to be paid on the first of every month: you are trying to ensure that rent is one of the first bills they pay. Rent is always paid in advance on the first of the month for the upcoming 30 day rent cycle.

I initially had a system where I would put a pink slip on the door if your rent was five days late. On the seventh day of the month, I would personally go and visit the tenants whose rent was late. On the fifteenth of the month, I would start the eviction process. Most of the tenants would find a way to get their rent in at that point. A notice from my attorney about eviction proceedings would let them know things were serious. With this process, tenants started to get programmed to the boundaries set and adhered to the system. Finding a system that works to get your rent payments in the bank before the tenth of the month is very important. Generally, my wife paid all the bills for the buildings around the twelfth of the month.

When you purchase a new building, invariably there will be someone ready to put you to the test. I looked at it as an opportunity to show the people how serious I was about rent being paid on time. On the seventh day of the month, I knocked on the door of one of my new tenants to inquire why the rent had not been paid. She looked me straight in the face and said, "I won't have the rent this month, Mr. Jenkins." I said, "What is the issue that has caused you not to have your rent?" She said, "I took my kids on a cruise because I believe poor people should be able to go on vacation just like anybody else." She added, "I will pay you a little extra every month until I am caught up." I said, "I think vacations are a great thing that most people want to do, but having a place to live is something that you need. I am not in the business of subsidizing vacations for my tenants, so I am going to evict you." I said, "We have a priority problem here."

She became very upset and started cursing me out, but I made my point to all the other tenants that unpaid or untimely rent would be met with negative steps toward eviction. After 30 days had passed in the eviction process, I put together a financial package to quickly get her out of the unit. I negotiated a 14-day move-out for seven hundred fifty dollars and a moving truck. The normal eviction time is 120 -180 days in DC, plus attorney fees. I really must show people the math before they understand that time is money. Again, I will do the math, rent is eight hundred fifty dollars a month, so I was out twelve hundred seventy-five dollars by her move-out day. It minimally takes 120 days to evict someone, costing thirty-four hundred dollars, and your attorney fees will be one thousand six hundred for an eviction. There are court fees, and you must pay about three hundred for the labor that comes with the sheriff. Getting tenants out within 45 days saved me over three thousand dollars and allowed me to fill the unit in 60 days, generating income for the sixty days that I would be dealing with a negative tenant.

I was forty years old and had the major responsibility of managing over thirty tenants at a time, along with administrative duties and maintenance responsibilities for the buildings. I was often reminded that I also had a wife and kids to raise at home. All the kids had different interests and hobbies, which felt like a full-time job. I had a demanding job as a Federal Agent, where I could be sent on assignment all over the United States at a moment's notice. The lack of sleep and the need to prioritize everything were habits I was accustomed to from my college days. In sports, there is a common phrase that says there are levels to everything. My limited time compelled me to crunch my schedule and reevaluate my priorities. It was a great situation to be able to integrate my dad into the system now that he had moved from Chicago. My management team had to increase their duties and handle a substantial amount more to free up tasks that I once did myself. Fortunately, the ability to pay people through electronic platforms saved me some valuable time as well.

For any business to be successful, effective time management or time allocation is the most important aspect of building any business. I prioritized my business because it was the engine driving all the great things I was able to do for my family, particularly regarding my kids' education. I really needed to try and balance things because I had a job and a family. At this time, my job as a Federal Agent suffered and received the least of my attention. I needed to keep my career because I truly took pride in being a Federal Agent, and I wanted to fulfill all the commitments I made when I raised my right hand and swore to serve. I often felt that there was not enough time in the day for me to put my best foot forward. During that period, I was working at Headquarters when a position became available that I thought I would like to pursue. Most coveted jobs in the government, such as a supervisory role, are usually already spoken for. The game plan was to perform very well in the interview so that my name would be spread around as someone who could excel in upcoming positions. I made the best-qualified list for the job and was given an interview date. However, my schedule became extra hectic with an upcoming addition to my real estate holdings the week of the interview. I was inundated with tasks that needed to be completed before the real estate closing. I had the worst luck because I was closing on the property at 9:00 a.m. and had my interview for a supervisory Special Agent position at 1:00 p.m. the same day. I arrived in the office from the closing with a sandwich in my hand at 12:30 p.m., just before my interview for a supervisory job. I have never performed well on any test that I was not well-versed or prepared for, and this was definitely the case for this interview. It was an underwhelming performance, to say the least; it simply was not enough time in a day, with all the balls I was juggling. I received an email from one of the supervisors on the panel who was saying he wanted to meet with me regarding my interview. I accepted the meeting out of curiosity because I knew I did not do well and had moved on. I arrived in this supervisor's office, and he told me to have a seat. He turned around and started looking at his emails again. After a few uncomfortable minutes I said I can reschedule the meeting for another day if you are busy. He said no just wait for me until I finish this up. I waited about five more minutes and then I stood up to leave because this was becoming a waste of time. He then turned around quickly and said have a seat because I wanted you to see how it feels when someone waste your time. He said I don't believe you spent any time preparing for an interview that was the most important thing in your life. That statement should have been the case, but it wasn't because I had just closed on a building putting one hundred and fifty thousand dollars of equity in my pocket.

He said I asked people about you, and they said you were sharp and was management material. He said you let them down and you let me down and I was very upset. At this point I had become angry, and it took everything in me not to tell him, I have an office too, but it's one that I provided for myself. My mind was racing, and I wanted to tell him that people call me Mr. Jenkins out of respect for what I have accomplished. I knew that wasn't the appropriate thing to say at that moment, so I simply replied, "I am sorry I wasted your time," and I left. We never spoke again, and he left the agency; I don't even know what happened to him. In retrospect, I grew to learn that time was too precious to waste, so I moved on and dismissed it as a bad delivery. Perhaps his intentions were good.

My cousin Spencer used to say, "If you give a job exclusive permission to feed you, they also have your consent to starve you. Keep several streams of income to protect yourself." At this point in my career, I was struggling with time management to reach my full potential as a father, business owner, and Federal Agent.

I drew wisdom from a story that happened to me one summer as a child visiting my grandparents in the deep South. I remembered how it made me feel when someone had consumed a large portion of something, leaving a lot less for me. My grandmother whose name was Girtherie made some of the best cobblers I have ever tasted. One Saturday evening she told me to go out in the yard and pick some black berries and she would make me a cobbler for Sunday dinner. I brought in a big bowl of black berries as she instructed me, and I was really anticipating gorging myself with the cobbler. In the deep South in the old days some preachers use to have two churches that they preached at. On first and third Sunday he traveled thirty miles to preach at my grandmother's church and on second and forth Sundays he preached at another church. On our way to church my grandmother Gutherie told me that it was the third Sunday, and the preacher traveled to preach, and it was her time to feed him after church. I was listening, but I was confused about how this information affected me until she mentioned the cobbler. I asked, "Excuse me, Grandma, what did you say about giving the Pastor our cobbler?" She replied, "Hush boy, we have to take care of the Lord's anointed man." She explained that the preacher loved her cobbler, so she wanted me to be patient and allow him to enjoy it first; we would eat and enjoy it afterward. The preacher was served a large plate of field peas, meatloaf, candy yams, and cornbread. As I watched him, I hoped he would say he was full as a tick on a dog and couldn't have the cobbler. After finishing his meal, he hit the table and said, "Sister Girt, I was hoping you might have one of those good cobblers around here." My grandmother squealed with laughter and delight, responding, "I sure do, Pastor; it's black berry. My grandson picked them fresh yesterday evening." He looked at me and nodded with a smile. The Pastor took his first helping of the cobbler and raved about how it melted in his mouth. I almost passed out when that old gluttonous Pastor asked for a second helping. I was furious watching him indulge in the cobbler. To make matters worse, he mentioned his wife's fondness for the cobbler, and my grandmother even sent him home with a little cobbler for her dessert. Finally, after he left, we had dinner. Afterward, Grandma pulled out the cobbler, but it was already half gone. She divided the remaining portions five ways for our family, and it was barely enough for one sufficient serving for me.

The cobbler is a representation of precious time that you want to prioritize. The glutinous Pastor could be an organization you belong to, your job or business that will take as much as you give them. I have seen so many Federal Agents lose their families because they let the job become that glutinous pastor taking everything leaving nothing for their kids. I can remember as a nine-year-old boy, the feeling of seeing a large portion of that pie eaten up before our family was in the equation. I knew that my buildings were the glutinous pastor for my kids. I did all that I could to make time for basketball games, gymnastics meets school plays. When you go over your schedule and you just can't find time for the people you once were social with, they think you have changed. People wanted me to participate in social events and volunteer for various activities; I had to explain that I would not be able to attend.

I often reflect on those memories in my life today, and it is evident that I was preoccupied with time. There are at least fifty phrases in the English language that involve time. If a young person shows me that he is obsessed with time, it captures my attention. The phrases I dislike the most are wasting time, passing time, and lost time. Conversely, I love terms like it's my time, on time, making time, and time is money. I dedicated an entire chapter to **time** because I want you to live life without regrets because it is an absolute fact that one day all of us, will be **"out of time!"**

Chapter 10
What would you do

I absolutely loved Southeast DC, and the people, as a whole, were salt-of-the-earth good people. I miss the sound of the horns and percussion playing to that Go-Go beat. The slang language and unique vernacular that the people used to communicate were infectious. The rhythm of the city reminded me of a slightly slower Southside of Chicago. What I loved most about Southeast was that everything was Black; it was the Chocolate City. Because of poverty, drug addictions, and a lack of education, sometimes you would see the darker side of the city. My tenants, from time to time, fell into those categories, and I had to deal with it. This chapter is really about putting yourself in these true scenarios and thinking about what you would do if you were the landlord. Would you evict them? Would you press charges? Would you fight, run, or just freeze up? One of my favorite songs back in the day was called What Would You Do. In that song, the guy asked the girl why she was out selling her body for money. She answered, "What would you do if your son was at home crying all alone on the bedroom floor because he's hungry? And the only way to feed him is to sleep with a man for a little bit of money, and his daddy's gone somewhere smoking crack, now in and out of lockdown? I ain't got a job now, so for you this is just a good time, but for me, this is what I call life." The song made me pause and have empathy for people who are trying to make it, hustling to make ends meet.

The first "What Would You Do" scenario is about "Sparkle." I was at one of my apartment buildings fixing the mailbox lock because one of the tenants lost her key and broke the lock to get into her mailbox. A gentleman came into the building, and he was looking at the names on the mailboxes. I said, "Sir, how can I help you?" He replied, "Excuse me, Brother, I am looking for a chick named Sparkle. She got big tits, and she gave me some great head last night in one of these apartments on the second floor." I was so surprised that I asked him to slow down and say who, and what he was looking for again. He repeated himself and added, "I got $75.00 more to give her." He said last night she made her son go next door with this older lady while they had sex. He said the little guy should be in school now; I felt bad getting him up like that. I said, "I am not sure who Sparkle is, but I am the landlord of this building, and prostitution is not allowed here." The guy left the premises without any further conversation. Now, I am a trained investigator, so I went for the weak link to find out the truth. I had a feeling who Sparkle was, but I had to make sure. I went and knocked on the older woman Mrs. Jackson's door and asked to speak with her in my office. I told her that it had come to my attention that she was part of a prostitution ring in my building. I said, "I am going to bring the police in and evict you if you don't tell me what's going on right now." She told me the young lady next door named Nicky was Sparkle. She said Nicky runs ads for sex, and when she gets a customer at night, she would pay her $15.00 to let her son sleep on her couch for an hour. The older woman begged me not to evict her. Next, I knocked on Nicky's door and asked her to come to my office and talk to me. I said, "Nicky, why are you selling your body in my apartment and bringing strange men around your seven-year-old son like that?" She jumped up and became very defensive, screaming and telling me I was lying about her. I said, "Young lady, sit down." I told her the story about the man. I said, "Please don't lie anymore because I already talked to Mrs. Jackson, and she gave it up." She sat down and began to cry, looking embarrassed and scared. She said, "Mr.

Jenkins, my son's father is doing five years, and I am trying to take care of my son the best way I can." I said, "Lady, go get a job! What is wrong with you?" At that moment, that song came to my head, and I calmed down. I said, "I am not going to put you out if you stop. This is dangerous, so please stop doing that because it is not safe for you, and it definitely will cause your son to have no respect for women."

Next a young couple moved into one of my nine-unit buildings. The woman came to fill out the paperwork and told me that a social service agency was paying seventy five percent of their rent. I was a little hesitant, but I felt like if I was getting seven hundred fifty from the agency and they were paying two hundred and fifty I could take a chance. When I met the husband, he told me that he was just getting out of rehab. He was a very friendly chatty fellow with big dreams of becoming a counselor. The couple seemed very happy, and they were going to church together and really trying to do this thing called life. One day I saw them walking down the street, so I pulled over to speak as I was leaving the building. I saw scratches on his face, and she had what looked to be a black eye. I drove away dismayed because I sensed things were changing for them.

Another sign was that they did not have the rent money for the month. This became a continuing theme for a couple more months. I was counseling them and giving them some compassion and latitude since I was getting the seven hundred fifty dollars. In the third month, I told them if they did not have their portion, I would let the social agency know and evict them. The next month, I came by on the fifth, and they asked me if I could please give them until the tenth of the month because the husband would be getting his check from his job. I came back on the tenth, and as I got to the door, I saw the husband staggering down the stairs. As he got closer to me,

I saw blood on his shirt with a knife handle sticking out of his stomach. I said, "Lean against the wall so that I can call 911 for help. What happened to you?" He said, "Mr. Jenkins, I messed up and spent the rent money on drugs. My wife and I got into a fight, and she stabbed me." She came downstairs crying and said, "I am sorry; I know I am going to jail." He said, "No baby, I love you; this is all my fault; I just need you to stay with me." The police and the ambulance came, and he did not want the police to arrest her. In the end, she wanted to go to the hospital with him in the ambulance. The police said she could not do that and put her in the police car. Soon after, I gave them a few dollars to move their belongings within two weeks.

Next, what would you do is about the liar! I was in my office in my "A" street Building. My office was located near the Adams apartment in the basement. I heard some bumping and screaming in the unit. I walked out and the door was half open where the noise was coming from. I pushed the door open fully to see what was going on. I saw Mr. Adams standing over his wife, and he was hitting her with his fist violently. I rushed in and pushed him to the side to move him off her. I said to him sternly, "Mr. Adams, if you don't calm down and stop hitting her, I am going to call the police and have you arrested." He said, "Mr. Jenkins, this no-good, conniving woman is the biggest liar in the world." He said she stole his money and gambled it away, and now she was lying about taking it. I stayed in the apartment for about 10 minutes to ensure that things calmed down before I left. About one year later, Mr. Adams died, and that's when it all started for me because I now had to get the rent money from Mrs. Adams. She came up with the most extravagant lies I have ever heard. One time, she told me that when she went to wash clothes, she left her door open while she went to put some clothes in the washer. She said she was talking to one of the other tenants at her door. She said while she went to put the clothes in the washer, someone broke into her unit and stole her rent money off the kitchen table. She said she called the police, but they would not arrest her. I called one of my friends at the police sixth district, and there was no action report for that address and no call into the station. On another occasion, Mrs. Adams called me and said, "Mr. Jenkins, I am telling you that I won't have your rent money." She told me that when she was walking home from the store, she fell on the ground and hit her head on the concrete.

Mrs. Adams stated that they called the ambulance to take her to the hospital emergency room. She claimed that either the ambulance personnel or the emergency room staff who attended to her stole her money orders. However, she could not produce a single piece of evidence that verified her visit to the emergency room. Let me emphatically state that I do not condone Mr. Adams beating his wife, but he certainly told the truth about her lying antics.

Her son stepped up to save his mother from being evicted by paying her rent. He said Mr. Jenkins ever since I was a kid my mother prided herself to be a scammer and the best liar in the world. The son said that is my mother and I will help her, but she will never change. That went on for a couple of years, but something happened, and he stopped paying her rent so again the antics began, and I finally evicted her lying self out of my building.

Now, what would you do about a repeat offender? A few years passed, and old Sparkle was back to her hustling ways. At this point, her son was about 10 years old, growing up fast and being exposed to more than he should have been. The young boy's father had recently been released from jail and started communicating with his son. One day, when Sparkle had a paying visitor, the boy called his father and informed him that his mother was in the room turning a trick and that he was sick of it. The boy's father arrived at the apartment armed with a gun, and the boy let his father into the unit. By that time, I had been working with the Metropolitan Police Department's Sixth District. To maintain a police presence, I had granted them permission to stage for police warrants near the target areas in my building's parking lots. My tenants were accustomed to seeing police cars pulling up and the teams donning their tactical gear and briefing for warrants. The police sergeant would usually give me a courtesy call if they were headed that way. I was sitting at my desk when I received a call from the sergeant, who informed me that we had a barricaded subject in my building. I left the office and went over to meet my colleagues from the Sixth District. Upon my arrival, I saw the negotiator speaking into Sparkle's door. I was briefed on the details: a man was in the unit with a gun, and a woman and a man were barricaded in the bedroom. I started to provide the negotiator with some background information. I overheard the negotiator tell the man that he would only worsen the situation if he committed any violent acts against the woman. After about an hour, the man was taken into custody and charged with being a felon in possession of a firearm. Sparkle and the man were brought out of the bedroom and interviewed about the barricaded incident. After the interview, I just sat there looking at Sparkle and said, "I am cool, but not that damn cool," and got up and left the building. On my way back to the office, I called my attorney and said, "Start the eviction process." I sent him the police reports to justify the eviction, which included all the facts, including charges of prostitution.

Next, what would you do about the five horsemen? During the complete refurbishment of one of my buildings, I noticed that, in the evenings, young people would gather in the parking lot, playing music. Two young women were essentially running a business, braiding hair for both women and men. I would sit by the window and listen to the music, reminiscing about my youth when we congregated, laughed, and talked together. For about two months, I felt that I had more pressing concerns about refurbishing the building than dealing with these young people. When the time came to start filling the units with potential tenants, I began to engage with the young people. They said, "We're not doing anything, and you don't have any tenants anyway." At that point, I had learned much more about handling situations correctly. I approached the police and requested their assistance in making them aware of the issues I faced with the young adults, which were hindering my chances of acquiring new tenants. After several weeks of pleading with these young people to stay out of my empty parking lot, I started having thoughts of how I had handled things in the past. I realized that I was taking the wrong approach and prayed for some law enforcement intervention. One evening after work, I was standing by the window, observing these young people having a party and braiding hair. Suddenly, I saw five police officers on horseback coming down the street. I ran down the stairs and stood at the front door of the building for a better view. The five horses entered the parking lot and chased the young people down the streets. Several of them were arrested after attempting to fight back. I had never witnessed such a sight before or after that day. The day these officers majestically appeared was the last day that these young people congregated in my parking lot. I was able to quickly schedule open houses with potential tenants looking at the building. This incident was pivotal for me in show casing the building in the best light.

Chapter 11
Go Get That Money

I often wonder what people see when they meet me, what my presentation is as a man. After an initial meeting with the Headmaster at Wakefield School, I was asked to meet with him again. He said, "Mr. Jenkins, this part of Virginia is horse country, and many of these students' parents' own horses. I overheard one of the parents mention having trouble getting their horse blankets cleaned. You seem to be an ambitious, smart man who could take advantage of something like that." I said, "Thank you for thinking of me. I will get back to you in a few days." I honestly had never heard of a horse blanket growing up in Chicago, but I was going to learn about it and "Go Get That Money."

I did some research by visiting the dry cleaners that many of the horse stables had used in the past. The older couple who ran the dry cleaners found the task of cleaning the horse blankets had become too labor-intensive for them. They told me that they kept raising the price to see if the customers would go someplace else, but they didn't. The older gentleman told me he charged one hundred and twenty-five dollars per blanket. I asked about cleaning solutions, and he told me about something he ordered online. Later, I was introduced to a parent with a horse stable, and I said, "I can pick up the blankets and clean them for eighty dollars a blanket." She said she had ten blankets and that was fine because she just passed the cost to the owner.

Through trial and error, I took the blankets early in the morning to an old, coin-operated bay car wash with a power spray gun. I took five of the blankets in my pickup truck, spread them out in the bay, and sprayed them down with the solution after wetting them. I waited about twenty minutes and then sprayed each blanket until it was clean. I took the wet blankets home and hung them up on my gate to dry. As you can imagine, that did not go over well in my upscale neighborhood, since my neighbors called the homeowners' association to complain. Once the blankets dried on the fence, I folded them, tied them with string, and delivered them to the horse stable. I was given a check for eight hundred dollars, and my expenses for gas and supplies were less than one hundred dollars.

Two days later, the woman with the horse stable called me back and said she was pleased with the service. She had called a few of her friends with horse stables, and they wanted me to contact them as well. I caught the full swing of entrepreneurial fever. She gave me about seven people to call, each of whom either personally kept their own horses or kept horses for other people. When I called these people, I had close to one hundred blankets to be done. I thought to myself, "I need to come up with a sound plan that I can execute to 'go get that money!'" Most horse owners only clean their blankets once or twice a year, so this is very seasonal income during the month of October. I divided the workload and went to get twenty-five blankets a week, laying them out on my grass in the backyard to dry. In two months, I had hustled and made about seventy-five hundred dollars, with less than three hundred in overhead costs. I could have stopped there, but I spent the entire winter thinking about how I could better prepare for the next fall horse blanket cleaning season.

I went to a local laundromat that had seventy-five-pound washers that could fit ten blankets at a time. I talked to the owner, asking if I could bring my horse blankets into his laundromat to wash and dry them. He said no because people would frown on washing their clothes after dirty horse blankets. I understood and went home to think of other ways to handle the situation. I came back and said, "When you close your laundromat at midnight, I will come in and pay you one hundred dollars an hour to keep it open. I will pay to utilize your large washers, and I will sterilize your machines when I am done. I will pay to run each machine empty to ensure no dirt is left behind." We had an agreement at that point.

Chemistry was certainly one of the classes I took in school that I thought I would never have any practical use for. I had made a promise to the laundromat owner that I would sterilize the washers after use. Using vinegar, bleach, or ammonia as a base was my first thought to get the job done. My knowledge of chemistry told me not to mix them because it could create a deadly gas. After experimenting, I purchased some pickle jars and made a formula with nine cups of ammonia, five cups of cheap laundry detergent, and a box of baking soda. This strong, potent mixture is what I used to clean the blankets and sterilize the washing machines.

The next year, I doubled the number of blankets I cleaned in just two weekends, staying up all night on Friday and Saturday and delivering them on Sunday. I was picking up and dropping off about two hundred blankets, so I raised my price to one hundred dollars. I think what the headmaster of the school saw was a young man determined to figure out a way to "go get that money!"

During the time when I was staying up all night and working hard to make sure my kids' tuition was paid, I thought about a story that my father-in-law Leon Edmond once told me. When I asked him if I could marry his daughter, he wanted to set a level of expectation with me. He told me that when my wife was attending an all-girls Catholic school in Chicago, his job at the steel mill closed. It was a high-paying job that he had enjoyed for twenty years, and suddenly it was gone. He said, "Emotionally, it was devastating, and I just sat at home for a month." He realized he had to move on, so he went out and started applying for other jobs. He was not able to get an interview, and things felt very bleak during that time. With a daughter in private school, he said, "I must go out and make something happen for myself." In Chicago, day workers stand in front of either Home Depot or White Castle to get picked up to work for the day.

He said he put his pride aside and went out early in the morning, standing beside migrant workers in search of work. Every day, he did this until one of the men who picked him up said, "I have a permanent position preparing the mortar for my bricklayers." The man continued, "It's hard work, but I will pay you well, and it will be consistent." My father-in-law worked for that man for a year until one of the warehouses he had applied to called to offer him a job. He said he was incredibly grateful to that construction owner because it meant his daughter could continue attending that private school.

He told me, "I'm sharing this story with you because I want you to understand my expectations for you as a man. No matter how much education and status you attain, I expect you to be able to 'Go Get That Money' by any legal means necessary." I could only imagine the level of humility it took for him to go out there and stand among those often seen as the lowest in our social order just to get work. I knew that I could never tell my wife's father that I couldn't find a job to feed my family, because he would never respect that. Expectations are important, but they are even more impactful when young people witness that work ethic firsthand.

During this period, I was in full entrepreneurial mode to "Go Get That Money." I purchased soda and snack machines to create multiple streams of income to cover my kids' sporting events and vacations. Anytime you're dealing with money, whether in large sums or small, it can be dangerous, so it's crucial to stay aware of your surroundings and take necessary precautions. I also purchased Automatic Teller Machines (ATMs), which required me to carry ten thousand dollars to fill each machine. I programmed my machines so that the most anyone could withdraw in a day was one hundred and fifty dollars, in ten-dollar bills. In the Black neighborhood, that was important because people would bypass other ATMs just to get to mine if they had twelve dollars. If they had ten dollars plus the two-dollar service fee, they could access their money. Ten thousand dollars in an ATM would last approximately two weeks to a month before it needed refilling.

In all my nine-unit buildings, I created laundry rooms by installing two coin-operated top-loaders and two coin-operated dryers in each basement, which provided auxiliary income. Once a month, I'd collect the money, and it was surprising to see that each building could generate two hundred and fifty dollars. One time, my daughter and I were heading to one of her AAU tournaments out of town, and I said, "Let's leave early so that I can stop by the buildings' laundry rooms to get us some spending money." She looked confused, and I didn't understand why until we got to the buildings. I took a bucket and emptied the coins into it from all the buildings. We went to the bank, exchanged the coins for cash, and I said, "Daddy got us five hundred dollars in spending money, so we can hit the road." She looked at me with a sad expression and said, "Daddy, why would you charge people to wash clothes when you know we don't pay to wash clothes at home?"

I replied, "Little girl, I paid for those washing machines, and I pay for the water and electricity, so they are just paying Daddy back." She said, "Okay, Daddy, but it still doesn't seem right." At the same time, she looked over at the bus stop and asked, "Why are all those people standing around on the corner?" I explained, "Airielle, that's called a bus stop, where people go to a designated spot to pay to ride." She said, "I thought everyone gets a car at sixteen, so why would they do that, Daddy?" Laughing, I asked, "So, you think a car is going to be handed to you on your sweet sixteen birthday?"

I was quiet for the rest of the drive to Pennsylvania, reflecting on how sheltered and entitled my kids were. Using a fruit analogy: no matter how great your fertilizer, soil, or irrigation is, if you don't pick the fruit when it's ripe, it will rot on the vine. As parents, our job is to provide all the advantages we can while they grow up, then let them face the world. If you grow up in an environment where all your needs and wants are met, you become comfortable—so comfortable that you expect your parents to ensure you maintain that level of comfort forever.

I felt a profound responsibility to provide a certain level of safety, comfort, and stability for my children so they could focus on their development as young adults. During my son Vendarryl Jr.'s freshman year in college, he couldn't take his car with him. I was quite amused when he complained about how horrible it was to wait at the campus bus stops like "poor people." I responded, "Young man, you are poor; your bank account is overdrawn—that's why I'm calling you."

I realized that there should be some balance to ensure my kids were hungry to make it on their own. We stand on the shoulders of men who were starving, but life has been too comfortable for my kids to even be hungry. I hoped that they were watching me and could duplicate the things I did in the future. Like most things that I do, I sat down and developed a plan to help them using the bicycle analogy. I helped them both learn to ride a bike by explaining the principles needed to successfully ride a bike. We started out with training wheels to practice those principles. Next, the training wheels came off, and I ran beside them with my hand on the seat to ensure they could balance the bike. After they gained the skills, at some point I let go and jogged closely behind. When they fell, I picked them up, dusted them off, and put them back on the bike. Soon after that, they were speeding down the street with the kids in the neighborhood. I sat down with both kids and explained that I wanted to see them succeed in life, and that would depend on what they did with their gifts. We spent some time together researching careers and came up with three that they felt they would excel in. I said, "Let's look at the salaries for these career fields because this will determine where you live, how often you can eat out, and the schools your children attend. I told them I would invest in their training for the career field if I felt like it was a good investment. If you show me that you don't appreciate my investment, I will pull it back for my enjoyment. My daughter said, "I like to play with babies, so I want to work in a nursery school." I said, "Baby girl, that's great, as long as you know that the pay is twelve dollars an hour. You will not be able to afford to drive the car you drive, live in this area, and, most importantly, you cannot live here after you finish college." People would say that I was being hard on my kids by telling them they were not welcome to live in my home after college. I believe if you do not set a goal for them, they will come home and become complacent. Early on, I did do some subsidizing for apartments, but they never came back home, and they are doing the first part—stabilizing a great W-2 job with upward mobility. My son called me recently and said, "Dad, I saw this building that we should look at purchasing." I excitedly said, "Let's talk about the particulars and get all the numbers, son." When he finally told me what was needed for the down payment, I said, "How much do you have of that, son?" He said, "I don't have anything, Dad, that's why I am calling you." I started laughing and said, "That is not the type of partnership that I engage in, son." To date, I would not quite call it a successful succession plan yet. I pray that in the future, the example my wife and I set before them will allow us to live to see them create other income streams and Go Get That Money!

Chapter 12
Losing The Y

A few years ago, I was on a work trip and had the opportunity to collaborate with a good friend I hadn't seen in years. I was excited to catch up with him about work, family, and my hometown, Chicago. However, I was shocked and disappointed when he told me that he and his wife were getting a divorce after 27 years of marriage. They had tied the knot around the same time as Shafonda and me, and our kids are about the same age.

He explained that their relationship had become centered around the kids—getting them to school, practices, and activities. When the kids were young, they argued but decided to stay together for the children's sake. Now that their kids are 26, 23, and 21, he said they no longer had a reason to stay together. Once they lost the "why" for being together, things became stressful and tough. The qualities he disliked in her were no longer things he could overlook.

I told him, "Thank God my wife and I are still doing well, but I'm struggling with another commitment now that the kids are gone." I continued, "I got into real estate to pay for private school and all the activities the kids were involved in. Man, God blessed me abundantly, and we were able to do great things. I would always tell my tenants, 'If you don't pay your rent, I can't pay my kids' tuition.' I made a big deal about needing that money for my kids."

Whenever real estate became tough, my reason for sticking with it—my kids—helped me push through the hard times. But now, with the kids grown (26, 23, and our "add-on kid," Eric, who's 29), I find myself questioning my purpose. When something goes wrong, I ask myself, *Why am I putting myself through this when my kids are grown?*

Anything you do for years—even marriage—can make you question why you continue. And you need a reason to stay. I told my friend how sad I was to hear that he and his wife had lost their reason. I asked him if he was sure about his decision, but I left it at that.

The "why" behind real estate for me was originally tied to paying for The Wakefield School in The Plains, Virginia. I wanted my kids to be prepared for the rigors of any university in the country. I believed in the culture and academics they experienced at that small school on the hill. Through The Wakefield School, Eric Wilson came into our lives. We became his host family, and he stayed with us for all four years he attended the school.

Many parents—whether they admit it or not—spend some time living vicariously through their kids. When I was a high school senior, I attended a college fair despite having already enlisted in the Air Force. At the fair, I noticed some young men wearing uniforms that said "Air Force." I walked up to them, introduced myself, and said, "I'm joining the Air Force right after graduation."

They responded, "We look forward to seeing you in Colorado Springs soon."

Confused, I replied, "No, my basic training is in San Antonio, Texas, for the Air Force."

One of them snickered and said, "You're going to be an enlisted soldier; we're going to be officers." They explained that the Air Force Academy is a highly selective college for future military leaders.

The next day at school, I went to my high school counselor's office and said, "I now know what I want to do after high school."

She replied, "I thought you were going into the military."

I said, "I want to go to the Air Force Academy now that I know it exists."

She gave me a knowing look and said, "Not with a 2.9 GPA, and no calculus or chemistry, you don't."

When she saw how deeply her words affected me, she softened her tone. "Sweetheart," she said, "you didn't take enough math or science courses to be competitive, and it's too late now. Follow your original plan: go into the military, get out, and then go to college."

I left her office feeling defeated, grappling with the painful realization of just how much I didn't know.

Eric came home from school one day during his junior year with a pamphlet about the Naval Academy Summer Camp. I was thrilled at the prospect of experiencing, through him, how the process might have unfolded if I had attended a school like The Wakefield School. Eric was a solid student, captain of the basketball team, and class president. I thought to myself, *Man, he has a great shot at getting into the Naval Academy.*

During his senior year, while he was away at a basketball tournament, a package arrived at our house from the United States Naval Academy. We immediately called him and excitedly said, "You've got a package here from the Academy!"

He eagerly replied, "Open it up for me!"

We tore the package open, and the moment we saw the word "Congratulations," we started screaming on the phone. The joy and excitement were overwhelming.

In 2015, Eric graduated from the U.S. Naval Academy in Annapolis, Maryland. Today, he is a Naval Officer living in Jacksonville, Florida, with a small but loving family.

MEKONG DELTA   I CORPS-DMZ   KHE SANH   HUE

While the kids were attending The Wakefield School, a teacher mentioned something during a parent-teacher conference that both amused and humbled us. He said, "I prepare differently for any class where Vendarryl Jr. is enrolled. If you miss even one fact, he will take over the class to show how smart he is." We realized we had to work with him to learn when to press the gas and when to ease off.

Two years after Eric left for college, my son, Vendarryl Jr., graduated at the top of his high school class and went on to attend the University of Virginia. As the premier public university in the state, UVA carried a culture and history I never imagined being part of our family's story.

At UVA, Vendarryl Jr. excelled. He became a student guide, was later elected Vice President of the University Student Judiciary

Committee, and ultimately earned a room on the Lawn—one of the most prestigious honors a UVA student can receive.

After graduating from the University of Virginia, Vendarryl Jr. continued his academic journey at Columbia University, one of the top Ivy League law schools in the nation. There, he connected with brilliant legal minds, further expanding his horizons. He even hosted U.S. Attorney General Eric Holder at an event, building an acquaintance with the prominent figure.

Today, Vendarryl Jr. is a civil rights attorney living in Washington, D.C., where he continues to make a difference.

VJ JENKINS
for HONOR

BLACK
CLASS
LAWYERS

I drove my kids to school every day to make sure I could pour into them. They jokingly called it the "Front Seat Blues" because they had to sit up front and listen to me tell stories and share life lessons all the way to school. Of all my kids, nobody got more "Front Seat Blues" than my daughter, Airielle. Growing up with two older brothers who were loud and argumentative, she became a quiet and unassuming young lady.

One day, when she was in fifth grade, she asked me to enroll her in a basketball camp. I hesitated and said, "No, sweetie. Daddy wants you to be a cheerleader, not a basketball player." But she was persistent, so I eventually signed her up. Lo and behold, we discovered her hidden superpower: she was a natural leader and an incredibly talented basketball player.

Airielle went on to lead The Wakefield School to two State Championship games and became the second-leading scorer in the school's history—boys or girls—with 1,433 points. She was a two-time first-team all-state player and a four-time all-conference player. After a couple of years playing college basketball, she began coaching and training kids, sharing her passion and skills with the next generation.

I'll never forget when one of the top AAU coaches in the area told her, during her sophomore year, "You might not be a born leader, but life has brought you to this position.

I've got four girls out here ready to run like thoroughbred horses, but I need a point guard to handle them. You came out here speaking softly and meekly, but I need you to take the reins and control these thoroughbreds."

That moment changed everything for her. She took the coach's advice to heart, and her leadership skills skyrocketed. From that day on, she never looked back.

After high school, Airielle graduated from James Madison University and later earned her master's degree in Hospital

Administration from George Mason University. She attended the Navy's Officer Development School in Rhode Island and is now a Navy Lieutenant working at the Navy Hospital in San Diego, California. Leadership, as it turns out, was always her calling!

THE PENTAGON
WASH
DEPARTMENT OF DEFENSE
UNITED STATES OF AMERICA

One afternoon, I came home from work and was helping my wife start dinner when my son, VJ, walked into the kitchen and asked me a question. "Dad," he said, "my friend told me that we're not authentic Black people."

His statement surprised me, but it also made me curious. Before I could respond, my daughter, Airielle, chimed in. She mentioned that a white girl on her basketball team had made a similar joke. Airielle recounted, "She said, 'It'll take you and another Black girl, Jessica, to equal one real Black girl,' and then laughed, saying, 'That's how white you live.'"

VJ jumped back in, adding his own experience. "My friend Harry said Black people live on the east side of town, but we live out west—in the white section of town—with a big house and three cars. He told me, 'You go to a prep school my parents can't afford, and you use really big words. There's nothing about that anyone would call Black.'"

I paused for a moment, gathering my thoughts, then replied, "Son, we are Black. We might be what some people call *Cosby Show* Cliff and Claire Huxtable Black, but we're still Black."

I continued, "When I was younger, Bill Cosby had a show where he played a doctor and had a beautiful, successful wife. Together, they raised their family in a nice home, with love and ambition. Some people looked at that show and thought, *That's not what Black families are supposed to look like.* But it was just as real as any other portrayal. We don't need to live up to anyone else's definition of what being Black means. Who we are—how we live—doesn't make us any less authentic."

Phylicia Rashad played an attorney on *The Cosby Show*. The Huxtables lived in a beautiful house, sent their kids to college, and shared the same love and laughter that I recognized in Black culture. Growing up, however, the only Black families I saw on TV were ones like the Evans family in *Good Times*—families struggling to escape the ghetto projects filled with stress, violence, crime, and strife.

That's what Harry associated with being Black because it was all he had seen on TV. His mind couldn't expand beyond what he perceived as reality from those depictions. But I knew better. I had read *Our Kind of People* by Lawrence Otis Graham and realized there were many Black families far more affluent than mine. I decided I needed to surround my kids with the socialization of upper-class Black society—groups like Jack and Jill, the Martha's Vineyard debutantes, and organizations such as the Alphas, Kappas, Sigmas, Omegas, AKAs, Deltas, the Links, and the Boule.

We cultivated a circle of friends who shared similar values. We played cards, barbecued together, and hosted dinner parties, giving our kids exposure to what I called "our kind of people" to help them feel confident and comfortable in those spaces. Today, Airielle is a member of the Links, and she and my wife love attending Link events together.

Real estate provided me with the opportunities to climb into another social level. However, as the years passed, it began to feel more like a burden than a blessing. It started taking time away from other pursuits. I began to wonder, *Why don't I cash out, invest the money, and enjoy life instead of spending my days dealing with buildings as I have for the last twenty years?*

One day, I had the option to take a scenic boat ride on the Potomac River or visit the buildings. I chose the buildings. When I got there, I found a clogged toilet in one unit, a broken window in another, and a leaking roof in a third. Standing by my car, I thought, *My kids are grown and out of college. Why am I still doing this? Why!*

It was in that moment I realized I had lost my "why." When you lose your why, the buildings suffer from mismanagement and disrepair because you no longer care enough to invest the time and energy they require. I met with my accountant and devised a plan to sell the buildings gradually, for tax purposes, and transition to a new chapter of life.

Now, we live as the modern-day Cliff and Claire Huxtable in our beautiful Huntsville, Alabama, spread!

We now live as the modern-day Cliff and Claire Huxtable in our Huntsville, Alabama, spread!

Chapter 13
Welcome Back

At that point in my career as a Federal Agent, I had served for 20 years. Yet, for much of that time, my real estate investments had been my primary focus. I had recently decided to push myself to the finish line in my career. Whether I would serve 25 or 30 years, I was determined to make the remaining time impactful.

One day, I was venting to one of my managers about the lack of experience and knowledge among the supervisors. He listened, then looked at me and said, "You have over 20 years on the job, and it's easy to complain. Why don't you become a supervisor?"

That wasn't the first time someone had said that to me, but for some reason, it struck a chord this time. I put my head down, worked hard, and a year later, I became a Supervisory Special Agent.

Over the years, I'd had a few great bosses and more than a few poor ones. From all of them, I learned valuable lessons—what to do and, just as importantly, what not to do. The bad bosses taught me how *not* to treat my people, a lesson I carried forward in my leadership.

Fate seemed to play a role when I saw a job opening in the same office where I'd started over 20 years earlier. I returned to Northwest Indiana—to East Chicago, Hammond, and Gary. When I arrived, I visited all the local police departments, including the state and county police. To my surprise, many of my old friends from local law enforcement were still there, now serving as Chiefs and Assistant Chiefs.

They were thrilled to see me. "I never thought you'd return to the area," they said, "but welcome back, brother." These were the same people who had helped me make solid cases as a young agent, and now we were back together, working as supervisors.

I had about 12 agents, six task force officers, and two secretaries working under me. One young agent came up to me one day and said, "You worked with my dad in this office years ago." That moment made me realize just how much time had passed.

Upper management gave me a clear mandate: transition the office to a more intelligence-led policing model. This approach faced significant resistance, as the agents in my office had achieved great success using confidential informants and police leads to build criminal cases. Despite the pushback, management requested an intelligence-led surge in targeted areas in Gary and East Chicago.

The surge involved a prolonged tactical enforcement deployment. We brought in a large group of agents to focus intensely on specific areas, producing measurable results that positively impacted the region. During this surge, I supervised about 35 agents.

One highlight of this time was working with my younger brother-in-law. Sixteen years younger than me, he had been just six years old when I started dating his sister. By the time we got married, he was ten, and we became close as he grew up through his pre-teen years and into college. We spent a lot of time together, and he looked up to me like a big brother. When he decided he wanted to become a Federal Agent, I was thrilled and supported him in any way I could.

At this point, he had 12 years on the job and was doing well. Having him on the surge team was a great experience, but it came with its moments. While it was easy for me to give him instructions, it was hard to hear him swearing casually with the guys. I had to remind myself that he was in his mid-thirties, not the little boy I once knew.

We picked out specific areas to target during the surge and achieved excellent results. I brought in several agents from other offices across the country who were experienced in the intelligence-led policing model. By working alongside these agents, my team began to see how the model could work in practice. Slowly, they became more willing to adapt and embrace the new approach.

Sometimes, events unfold that cement your leadership ability and earn the respect of your team. During the surge, we developed a case on a documented serial shooter affiliated with a Latin gang. This individual had killed several people and vowed to shoot to the death rather than return to jail. Upper management decided to bring in our SWAT team to make the arrest, but there was a slight delay in getting them into place. In the meantime, I was tasked with conducting a 24-hour surveillance of the suspect. I had enough manpower to cover the surveillance, so we organized shifts and started that night. I was explicitly instructed not to attempt the arrest, only to monitor the suspect.

The next day, I received a call from one of my agents saying the suspect had been dropped off at a tent rental job by his girlfriend. The agent sent me a photo of the suspect wearing red shorts and a tank top. Judging by his attire, I felt confident he wasn't armed. I saw this as a rare opportunity to make the arrest without incident.

I left the office and came on-site to evaluate the situation firsthand. I gathered my team and told them, "Listen, I'm the on-scene commander. If I see an opportunity to make the arrest without incident, I will." The agents looked shocked and asked, "Are you sure, boss? Weren't you told not to make the arrest?"

I replied, "I'm here on the scene, and I can see things they can't. We'll proceed if the opportunity is right."

We continued the surveillance until the suspect went to Home Depot to buy supplies for a tent installation. As he was loading the supplies into his truck, I gave the takedown signal. My agents moved in quickly and arrested him without incident.

The arrest landed me in some hot water with the front office, but my team saw it differently. They appreciated working for a leader willing to make a tough call under pressure. After that, they began saying, "That guy has the guts to make the hard decisions—he's the kind of boss you want to work for."

One particularly memorable situation occurred when an agent from Arizona, newly assigned to my team, came into my office and said, "Boss, I can't stay here. It's cold, and I don't like this area."

I empathized but responded, "You've been sent to me for a 90-day deployment. You can either embrace it and make the best of it, or fight it and be miserable."

Recognizing his struggle, I made an effort to support him. I invited him to lunch a couple of times a week early on to provide some encouragement and counseling. By the end of the 90 days, as we were wrapping up the assignment, he came into my office with a surprising announcement.

"I've requested another 30 days to help you close everything out," he said. "I've really enjoyed working for you and don't want to leave. But my wife says I'm going crazy and need to get back to Arizona."

I smiled and replied, "I appreciate that, but your wife is the real boss, so you'd better get back to Arizona."

During my time supervising in Indiana, my group achieved significant success. We won several awards, including an Organized Crime Drug Enforcement Task Force (OCDETF) award, and several of my agents earned TOP COP awards and bonuses. This period proved to me that once you learn to excel, the skills become transferable to other endeavors.

Throughout my career as a Federal Agent, I had achieved many milestones: I became a Crisis Negotiator, a Polygraph Examiner, an Interviewing Instructor, and, eventually, a Supervisory Special

Agent. However, there was one goal I had yet to fulfill—returning to the academy, the place where so many opportunities had first opened for me.

My supervisor wrote me a glowing letter of recommendation, highlighting my leadership skills, and I was selected to serve as a class supervisor for a group of 50 young agents. When I drove up to the academy gate, a wave of nostalgia hit me. I recalled all the anxious feelings I'd had 25 years ago: *Do I belong here? Will I pass? Is this moment too big for me?*

As I handed my credentials to the person at the gate, they looked at my badge, saw "Supervisory Special Agent," and said, "Welcome back, Sir."

I smiled and replied, "I guess no two days are alike."

I met my class on Monday morning as they prepared for their initial physical fitness qualification. During training, the trainees were not yet agents—they were treated as if they were on the brink of becoming part of something great. I wanted them to feel like they were a team, working together to navigate the challenges of the academy.

I remembered how I felt as a minority trainee, not knowing anyone and feeling isolated. To foster unity, I introduced them to the term "Team America." I told them, "From now on, we work as a team, study as a team, support each other as a team, and celebrate as a team. We are Team America."

The academy staff didn't quite know what to make of it. The camaraderie created by this simple name was immediate and profound. The section chief called me into his office one day and asked, "What the hell is Team America, and how did you come up with that?"

I explained, "In the field, we work with informants who often want to feel like they're part of something bigger—part of the law enforcement team. I came up with the idea of giving them a T-shirt that said *Team America.* When I handed it to them, they'd work harder and stay loyal because they felt included. *Team America* is about being part of something meaningful."

He chuckled and said, "Man, get out of my office. You're full of it, but I see it works."

As I looked around the classroom, I couldn't help but notice that the demographic hadn't changed much in the 25 years since I'd been a trainee. Back then, there were three Black trainees, two females, one Asian, one Hispanic, and forty-three White males. This class was slightly more diverse, with four Black trainees, three White women, and forty-three White men.

I reflected on my own experiences at the academy, particularly my struggles with firearms. I had no prior experience, and the learning curve was steep. Fortunately, my sports background helped me adapt. I practiced every night, dry firing like I had practiced jump shot mechanics. I barely passed the firearms qualification, but I passed.

One particular memory stood out. During my time at the academy, there was a young Black woman in my training class who failed her firearms qualification. Her final re-qualification was scheduled for 48 hours later—on her birthday. If she didn't pass, she would be escorted out of the academy and fired. I was determined not to let that happen. I told her, "Let's go to work."

After class, I took her to an outside gun range and discovered that she could shoot well. The problem was the technique the instructors were teaching—it was throwing her off and causing inconsistency. I told her, "For the qualification tomorrow, shoot the way you're comfortable to pass, and then practice the new technique afterward."

I knew the academy supervisors and firearms instructors already had her paperwork ready to escort her out. I just smiled to myself because I was confident she would pass. On the day of her re-qualification, they made her shoot in front of the entire class—a stressful situation for anyone. She stayed focused, ignored the yelling from the firearms instructor, and shot the way she was comfortable. To no one's surprise but theirs, she passed.

The firearms instructor was angry and scolded her for not using the technique he had taught. I stepped in and said, "Calm down. She chose to live to fight another day. She'll learn your technique over time." Her classmates celebrated her success, and I bought her a birthday cake. We sang "Happy Birthday" to her, turning what could have been a devastating day into one of triumph.

In the end, every trainee in the class I had dubbed "Team America" passed the academy—a rare accomplishment.

I headed back to Washington, D.C., to tend to my properties after managing my business from another state for three years. At the time, I was serving as the Program Manager for International Affairs for my agency. Part of my role involved overseeing international training facilities where U.S. law enforcement trains foreign police. These facilities are located in San Salvador, El Salvador; Budapest, Hungary; Bangkok, Thailand; and Gaborone, Botswana, Africa. Visiting these places as a diplomat for the United States government felt like an incredible honor for a kid from the south side of Chicago.

However, the frequent trips, with flight times exceeding 18 hours, began to take a toll after a year. I was later asked to conduct training in the CARICOM countries, the Caribbean Community.

This experience had a profound impact on my personal life, as I visited places deeply connected to the African diaspora: Antigua, the Bahamas, Barbados, Dominica, Jamaica, Grenada, Guyana, Haiti, Saint Kitts, Suriname, and Trinidad and Tobago.

Training police officers in these countries felt different because, for the first time, everyone in the classroom was Black. I recall teaching a class in Barbados and giving the officers a 15-minute break. After 20 minutes, I went looking for them and found them engrossed in an intense card game, with the rest of the class standing around watching. I said, "Get back to class so I can finish my lecture!" But deep down, I thought, *Man, Black people are culturally similar to Black Americans in so many ways.*

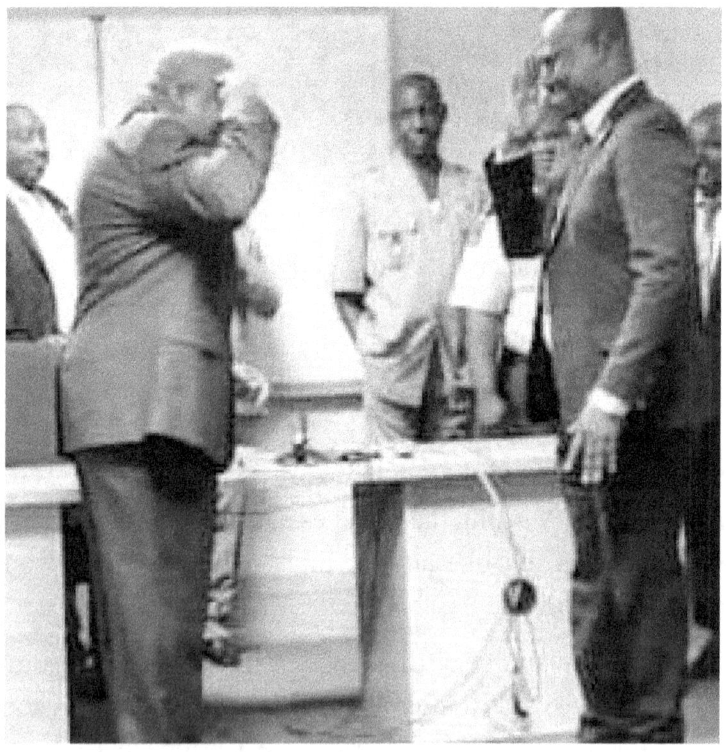

During my time there, I became convinced that Black people should never live anywhere coconuts aren't available. I started every morning with fresh coconut water and ate the jelly inside for breakfast. When I asked the officers why I didn't see any White officers, they replied, "We've only had two White police officers in our history." If it weren't for the frequent electricity blackouts, high gas prices, and poor healthcare systems, I might have seriously considered retiring in the Caribbean.

By January 2019, I had decided it was time to retire from my role as a gun-toting Supervisory Special Agent. For my final international trip, I paid for my wife's ticket so she could join me on a farewell journey to Botswana, Africa. We arrived early to experience a safari in South Africa—a once-in-a-lifetime adventure. Being out there with the animals in their natural environment was mesmerizing. Lions, elephants, rhinos, giraffes, antelopes, and countless other species roamed freely around us. The guide reassured us, saying, "The animals recognize the jeeps and won't attack, but please don't get out of the jeep unless I say so."

When I checked into the school at the Gaborone International Law Enforcement Academy, I informed them this would be my final trip abroad for the government. The head of the school surprised me, saying, "We're going to have a retirement celebration for you." I laughed and replied, "Thank you, but back home, my people are just going to have cake and punch in the conference room. I appreciate this, though!"

On the last day, after I finished teaching, the students lined up to speak to me. One by one, they shared heartfelt words that moved me deeply. Many told me, "You are our brother who was taken away from home. We are so happy you have returned, and we want to say, 'Welcome back.' Please come again to see your people."

Their words struck a powerful chord. As they hugged me, I responded emotionally, "I have been gone for 400 years, and I thought you had forgotten me." They laughed and said, "No, my brother, you are home."

The celebration that followed was fit for a king. There was a grand feast, and dancers performed with such energy and joy. At one point, they pulled my wife into the circle, and she danced alongside her African brothers and sisters. Watching her, I couldn't help but smile and think, *We're living an extraordinary life for two kids from Chicago.* I leaned over and said to her, "What a beautiful way to end this chapter of our lives—celebrating in Africa with our people."

Epilogue

While I was in college at Chicago State University, I worked with my father on 47th and State in Chicago. Next to the tire store where I worked, an old man named Joe Ferguson owned a shoe shop that he had run for over fifty years at that location. Over time, Joe and I grew close. He had been testing me subtly for a while, trying to see where my head was at.

One day, Joe asked me, "Have you ever heard of the term *the talented tenth*?"

I replied, "W.E.B. Du Bois' *The Negro Problem*. It's a term that speaks to the responsibility of the leadership class of African Americans in the 20th century."

Joe nodded and said, "You know W.E.B. Du Bois was the first Black man to graduate from Harvard with a Ph.D., but that doesn't mean only the most educated people are destined to lead. We need regular people who are leaders to step up and take charge. You must be a servant leader—someone willing to shine your light for those who live in the dark."

Joe then shared some of his own history. "I came to Chicago in the late '40s as a young man from the South. Back then, youngblood, everybody wore sharp suits, top hats, and always had nice shoes. When you came up from the South, Chicago had meatpacking plants, steel mills, and trades like bricklaying and plumbing. Everybody was working and earning enough to take care of their families."

He paused, a nostalgic look in his eyes, and added, "There was a father in almost every house, and families went to church together. But on Friday and Saturday nights, man, Chicago came alive. The jazz clubs, the blues clubs, the nightclubs—it was really a jumping city."

I smiled and asked, "What happened? Because all I see now are crackheads running around here."

Joe sighed and said, "Let me give you an example from my life so you can understand." He continued, "My son went off to fight for his country in Vietnam. While he was over there, he saw some horrible things—things no young man should ever see. To cope with the pain, he and his friends started messing with heroin, just to get through the days. When my son came home, he was addicted to drugs. His wife left him, took the kids, and moved into the housing projects."

Joe paused, his voice heavy with emotion. "When my son finally got clean and tried to get his family back, his wife told him she couldn't risk losing her housing voucher by trusting a drug addict again. The government had become their father, providing food stamps and housing. By the '80s, the streets were full of young people walking around with crack pipes. And the young men who profited from their people's pain by selling it? They ended up with long jail sentences."

Joe leaned back and looked at me. "Youngblood, America has had a big problem on its hands ever since 1865—figuring out what to do with all these descendants of slaves. Back then, if a slave got caught trying to read, they got thirty lashes on their back. Most of them lived and died in ignorance."

I nodded and said, "The 13th Amendment was ratified on my birthday—December 18, 1865. I was born exactly one hundred years later, in 1965."

Joe looked at me with a thoughtful expression. "One hundred years is not a long time," he said.

"I realize that," I replied. "My great-granddaddy, Phil Agee, was born a slave in 1861. My grandfather, Cleveland, was one of his eleven kids, born in 1911. My mother, Annetter, was born in 1941. She got out of Alabama as quickly as she could, heading to Chicago in 1959. And I came along in 1965."

Joe placed his hand firmly on my shoulder. "I'm an old man now, Youngblood. I'm about to close this store, but let me tell you something. You've got to be an 'old Joe' to somebody. Shine your bright light and help guide your people. That's what W.E.B. Du Bois meant when he talked about the *talented tenth*. It's not just about education or success—it's about serving your people and lifting them up."

Joe's words have stayed with me over the years. Whenever I speak in schools or mentor groups through organizations like the 100 Black Men of America or Alpha Phi Alpha, Inc., I think of old Joe Ferguson. We all stand on the shoulders of men like him—men who have gone on to glory but left their wisdom for us to carry forward.

I hope that my life's work and this book can be a light that shines brightly, guiding someone from the darkness into the light. We all should carry a little Harriet Tubman within us because there are still people out there we need to reach back for and bring forward.

~Vendarryl Jenkins Sr.

www.ingramcontent.com/pod-product-compliance
Lightning Source LLC
Chambersburg PA
CBHW071433130726
47997CB00006B/2069

them the light bulb came on too late. It made me happy when a young person would say with a look of amazement, sir, do you own this big building. I knew what they thought was impossible, suddenly became possible. I mentor young people mainly in high school and college, but writing a book called "Zero to One Million" allows me to expand that number exponentially. Having the mantra to live an extraordinary life changes the trajectory of a young person's life aims. I also realize that it's not just the school subjects taught, it is the injection of the level of extraordinary possibilities you aspire to. The talented tenth in our society need to shine their lights for people who live in darkness.

ABOUT THE AUTHOR

Author retired after 28 years as a Supervisory Special Agent with the Department of Justice and is now living in Huntsville, Alabama. A real estate investor for over 20 years in the Washington DC Area. From Chicago Illinois. Proud member of Alpha Phi Alpha Fraternity Inc. and 100 Black Men of America. Veteran US Air Force, BA in Business Administration from Chicago State University. MS in Criminal Justice University of Wisconsin Platteville.

ISBN 979-8-89406-384-3